RECORDS
OF
THE GUPTA DYNASTY

RECORDS
OF
THE GUPTA DYNASTY

ILLUSTRATED BY

INSCRIPTIONS, WRITTEN HISTORY, LOCAL TRADITION, AND COINS.

TO WHICH IS ADDED A CHAPTER ON THE ARABS IN SIND

BY

EDWARD THOMAS, F.R.S.,

LATE OF THE EAST INDIA COMPANY'S BENGAL CIVIL SERVICE; CORRESPONDANT DE L'INSTITUT DE FRANCE; CORRESPONDING MEMBER OF THE GERMAN ORIENTAL SOCIETY; MEMBER OF THE ROYAL ASIATIC SOCIETY; HONORARY MEMBER OF THE ASIATIC SOCIETY OF BENGAL; MEMBER DE LA SOCIETE ASIATIQUE DE PARIS; AND MEMBER OF THE NUMISMATIC SOCIETY OF LONDON.

GYAN

Published by

Gyan Publishing House
5, Ansari Road
Daryaganj, New Delhi-110002
Phone: 011-47034999, 9811692060
E-mail: books@gyanbooks.com

Distribution Network
gyanbooks.com
India, USA, Canada, UK, Australia, France

ISBN : 978-81-212-2804-6 (HB)
First Published, 1876

2nd Impression 2021

Printed at: Gyan Press, Delhi.

Records of the Gupta Dynasty
Author: Edward Thomas

RECORDS

OF

THE GUPTA DYNASTY.

ILLUSTRATED BY

INSCRIPTIONS, WRITTEN HISTORY, LOCAL TRADITION, AND COINS.

TO WHICH IS ADDED A CHAPTER ON THE ARABS IN SIND.

BY

EDWARD THOMAS, F.R.S.,

LATE OF THE EAST INDIA COMPANY'S BENGAL CIVIL SERVICE;
CORRESPONDANT DE L'INSTITUT DE FRANCE; CORRESPONDING MEMBER OF THE GERMAN ORIENTAL SOCIETY;
MEMBER OF THE ROYAL ASIATIC SOCIETY; HONORARY MEMBER OF THE ASIATIC SOCIETY OF BENGAL:
MEMBRE DE LA SOCIÉTÉ ASIATIQUE DE PARIS; AND MEMBER OF THE
NUMISMATIC SOCIETY OF LONDON.

LONDON:—1876.

CONTENTS.

PREFATORY NOTE.

THE subjoined Memoir on the obscure annals of the Gupta Kings of India was undertaken, in the first instance, with the limited purpose of describing Mr. Burgess's newly-acquired coins in the pages of his Archæological Report for the season of 1874–5.

Circumstances connected with his return to India, and the incidentally-delayed calls for MS., have enabled me to revise and amplify several sections of my original text; others, wholly or partially set up in type, have been retained in their outline form; while, latterly, important notes, which would have required time to complete, have been deferred for future publication, so as to avoid any interference with the progress of the Editor's leading Report, already somewhat in arrear.

A brief notice of some Muhammadan coins—obtained on the same occasion—which illustrate the transfer of Ethnic supremacies in the valley of the Indus, concludes these independent Chapters.

GUPTA AND SURASHTRAN COINS.

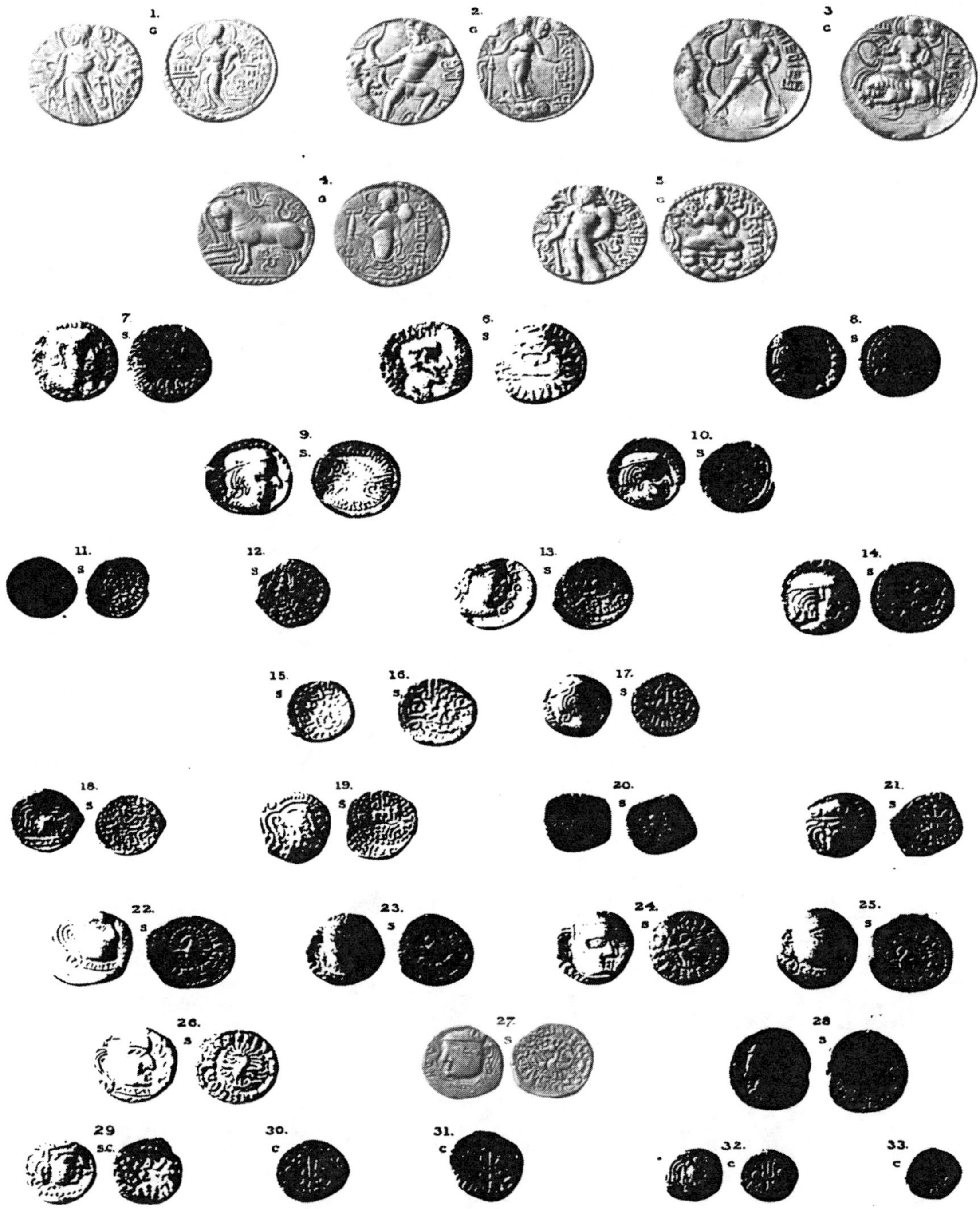

SÂH AND GUPTA COINS, &c.

Mr. Burgess, during his late tour, succeeded in obtaining some very interesting specimens of the coins of the local Ṣáh kings of Suráshtra and their imperial Gupta successors which he has requested me to describe.*

I have taken advantage of the opportunity to arrange and classify in the accompanying autotype plate, contrasted examples of the various provincial currencies of the latter dynasty, and I have attempted, in a general way, to collect the extraneous data bearing on the still obscure history of a race, whose domination forms so important an epoch and hitherto undefined time-mark amid the dynastic revolutions of India within itself. This may be held to be a very bold expansion of a text based upon a handful of coins, but Numismatic studies I have always maintained, when properly and scientifically treated, open out a very large and expansive circle of investigation.

In the present instance there have unfortunately been few opportunities for systematic arrangement, or for the ordinary completion of details; but, incidentally, where coins have proved their leading title I have admitted them into the front rank, in which prominent position I can usually sustain them, when their rough edges preserve but fair traces of the marginal legends of the original die, and when the native engravers have not subsided into ignorant and mere mechanical imitators of device and superscription.

The materials available for the determination of the age and the spread of the dominions of the Guptas seem to arrange themselves in the following order :—

a. Inscriptions.

b. Written history.

c. Tradition.

d. Coins.

a.—Inscriptions.

The genealogy of the Gupta family has been singularly well-preserved, considering the limited range of their extant inscriptions and the persistent oblivion to which their successors would, perhaps designedly, have consigned them.

The earliest of these, in point of time, is the Allahábád manifesto of Samudra Gupta, the fourth in succession of an ancestry claiming little pretension to renown, and the second only in the order of kings, who attained anything beyond restricted celebrity.

---

* A slight difference will be observed between the system of transliteration employed in the following pages and that followed by Mr. Burgess. The chief departure from his usage is in the marking the श by ṣ, in preference to the unsightly ś. My theory is, that dots *below* the line should, as far as possible, constitute the discriminating mark for consonants, and that accents *above* the line should be reserved for vowels. I prefer the acute accent ′ to the circumflex ^ as less disfiguring to the vowel letter, a disadvantage inherent in the ^, and especially detrimental in maps.

This first heir to an imperial father took advantage of a ready prepared monolith, to supplement, in the writing current in his day an account of his own rise, in the form of a quasi palimpsest,* attached to the original contemporary palæograph in the old square *láṭ* character in which Aṣoka, in the twenty-seventh year of his reign (B.C. 232), had proclaimed, unwittingly, his undeveloped Buddhistic tendencies, and his advocacy of the more simple doctrines of mercy to animals, the preservation of animal life, and the alleviation of animal woes.†

The second record of the Gupta heritage, likewise perpetuated on stone, is to be seen in the Mathurá inscription from the Katrá mound, wherein Samudra's parentage is apparently repeated in accordance with the tenor of the earlier monument.‡ The genealogy of the family is further extended in the inscription on the Bhítari *láṭ* or monolith, in the district of Gházipúr and in its counterpart at Bihár,§ which carries the succession down to Skanda Gupta and an unnamed heir.||

From these inscriptions the recognised line of kings may be restored after the following order:

The Gupta Kings.

1. *Mahárája* Ṣrí Gupta.
2. *Mahárája* Ṣrí Ghaṭotkacha.
3. *Mahárájádhirája* Ṣrí Chandra Gupta.
4. ,, Ṣrí Samudra Gupta.
5. ,, Ṣrí Chandra Gupta II.
6. ,, Ṣrí Kumára Gupta.
7. ,, Ṣrí Skanda Gupta.

The family tree, originally reconstructed by Dr. Mill,¶ is of importance, in the present inquiry, as showing the moderately advanced position of the early members of the so-called regal line:—

1 Gupta.

2 Ghaṭotkacha. Lichchavi, a private Rájput, whose daughter was

3 Chandra Gupta—+—Kumára Deví, wife of the king. Sanhāriká, an independent princess, whose daughter was

4 Samudra Gupta *Rája and Sovereign* { ——+——(¹) A Queen, name unknown, ——+——(²) Deví, daughter of Mahádaitya.

5 Chandra Gupta II.

6 Kumára Gupta.

7 Skanda Gupta.

8 A young prince (Mahendra Gupta?), a minor at the date of this inscription.

---

* *Journ. As. Soc. Beng.* vol. III. p. 105; vol. VI. p. 978; *Journ. Bom. Br. R. As. Soc.* (*revision by Bhau Daji*), vol. IX. p. cxcvii.; Prinsep's *Essays*, vol. I. p. 233.

† My *Ancient Indian Weights*, Marsden's (International) *Numismata Orientala*, London, 1874, p. 27.

‡ General Cunningham's *Archæological Report*, vol. III. plate XVI. No. 24, p. 37.

§ *Journ. As. Soc. Beng.* 1866, p. 271; *Journ. Bom. Br. R. As. Soc.*, 1871–2, p. 59, Bhau Daji's *revised reading*; Cunningham's *Archæological Report*, vol. I. pl. XVII. p. 38, and pl. XXX. p. 94.

|| *Journ. As. Soc. Beng.* 1836, p. 661; Prinsep's *Essays*, vol. I. p. 240.

¶ Dr. Mill, *Journ. As. Soc. Beng.* vol. III. p. 344; Prinsep's *Essays*, vol. I. pp. 235, 243, 245.

Much emphasis has been laid by some modern commentators* on the appearance of the words *Sháhán Sháh* in the Samudra Gupta inscription at Allahábád, above quoted, as tending to prove that the Guptas must have been contemporary with the Sassanian kings of Persia (226–632, A.D.). I wish to rectify any such misapprehension, as the point is of real importance as collateral evidence. I have from the first contended† that this title was in nowise exclusively the property or impress of the Sassanian family. We have the *Khsháyathiya Khsháyathiyánam* of Darius,‡ and the counterpart ΒΑΣΙΛΕΥΣ ΒΑΣΙΛΕΩΝ with the *Rajaraja* and *Adhiraja* of the Bactrian or rather Indo-Scythian coins.§ We can now further cite the existence of a *Shahíyah* dynasty in Khárizm of the race of Cyrus,‖ and point to the more immediate testimony of our Mathurá inscriptions, where Vásudeva is designated as *Sháhi*, and, in other epigraphs, by the parallel *Devaputra*, which reappears in conjunction with the *Sháhán Sháh* on the Allahábád column — combinations, which would preferentially indicate the continued rule of some members of this Scythic race in outlying portions of their old dominions.

It does not form part of the immediate object of the present résumé, to examine the entire series of the Gupta inscriptions, but the following passages have been selected as furnishing authentic dates, applicable, as other data may chance to sanction, to the general determination of the Gupta place and epochal position in Indian history.

No. 2. Inscription of Chandra Gupta.¶

The short inscription at Udayagiri contains the name of Chandra Gupta under the title of "*Parama-bhattáraka Mahárájádhirája*," and the date of *Samvat* 82 [in figures] 11th of the bright half of Ṣrávana.

*No. 3. Inscription of Chandra Gupta.***

The inscription on the eastern gate at Sanchí, near Bhilsa, commences, "To all respected Ṣramanas, the chief priests of the *ávasatha* ceremonial . . . The son of Amuka, the destroyer of his father's enemies, &c. . . . obtaining the gratification of every desire of his life through the favor of the great emperor Chandra Gupta

---

* Cunningham, *Bhilsa Topes*, p. 147; Lassen, *Ind. Alth.* vol. II. p. 752, &c.; Fergusson, *Journ. R. As. Soc.*, vol. IV. p. 108.

† On the Epoch of the Gupta Dynasty, *Journ. As. Soc. Beng.* (1855), vol. XXIV. p. 387; Prinsep's *Essays*, vol. I. pp. 272, 274. See also vol. II. pp. 109, 110, and *Journ. R. As. Soc.*, vol. XII. pp. 341–344; *Ariana Antiqua*, plates XVI.–XVII.

‡ *Journ. R. As. Soc.* vol. X. p. 195; Scythic, *Kokofainna*, vol. XV. p. 95; Persian variant *Naqa Naqayánám*, p. 159.

§ Prinsep's *Essays*, vol. II. pp. 205 *et seq.*

‖ "Abu Rihán further speaks of the Kharizmian writing and records, which were carefully investigated by Kotaibah Ibn Moslem when he conquered the country, and strengthens the authority of these native documents, by showing that a single family, named the Shahíyah, and supposed to be derived from Cyrus, had reigned in Kharizm—with the exception of a Turkish or Scythian interregnum of ninety-two years—from the Achæmenian period down to the time of the Mahommedan invasion."—Sir H. Rawlinson, *Central Asia*, London, 1875, p. 246.

¶ Cunningham, *Bhilsa Topes*, p. 151; Prinsep's *Essays*, vol. I. p. 247.

** *Journ. As. Soc. Beng.*, vol. VI. p. 455, plate XXV., and vol. VII. p. 455; Prinsep's *Essays*, vol. I. p. 246.

. . . . . has given, &c. as an act of grace and benevolence of the great emperor Chandra Gupta, generally known among his subjects as Deva Rája (Indra). . . . .

"In the *Samvat* year 93 [in figures], Bhádrapada 10th."*

No. 4. Translation of an Inscription on the Monolith of Kuhaon, in the Gorakhpúr division, N. W. P., India, by Babu Rajendra Lála.

"The year 141 having been over (or the close of the year 141), and the month of Jaishṭhya having arrived, the empire of Skanda Gupta—the floor of whose audience chamber had been swept by gusts from the bowing of the heads of kings by hundreds; sprung from the line of the Guptas; of wide extended fame; opulent beyond all *others*; comparable with Ṣakra; lord of hundreds of monarchs."†

No. 5. Translation of an Inscription of the time of Skanda Gupta, on a copper-plate grant found at Indor, near Anupshahar on the Ganges.‡

"Amen; may he, whom Brahmans, in obedience to law, bepraise with the harmony of meditation and the entire devotion of their minds . . . be your protection!"

"In the year 146, in the month of Phálguna, the — (?) of the thriving and invincible kingdom of his most noble majesty, the supreme sovereign of great kings, the auspicious Skanda Gupta, for the promotion of prosperity in the possession of the owner Sarvanága in Antarvedi (or the Doáb of the Ganges and Yamuná)."§

No. 6. Inscription of Skanda Gupta on the Northern face of the Girnár rock. ||

"To the perfect one, Vishṇu, who snatched from Bali for the happiness of Indra," &c. "Afterwards he . . . who by his own arms obtained glory (*parákrama*), and who is the most distinguished of kings," . . . "may he, Skanda Gupta, be glorious" . . . (the text goes on to detail Skanda Gupta's difficulties in the selection of a fit ruler for Suráshtra and his ultimate choice of) Parṇadatta" . . . (who delegates his authority to his son) "Chakrapálita." . . . "Afterwards, when in the course of nature the rainy season arrived . . . the lake Sudarṣana burst (its embankments). When a century of years *plus* thirty passed, in the sixth day of Bhídrapada, at night, counting from the era of Gupta" (*Guptasya kála*).

(Seven years seem to have elapsed before its repairs were either commenced or fairly advanced when a record appears) "for the benefit of the king and of the city, in a

---

* Prinsep's *Essays*, vol. I. p. 246.

† *Journ. As. Soc. Beng.* vol. VII. p. 37; Prinsep's *Essays*, vol. I. p. 250; *Journ. As. Soc. Beng.* 1861 p. 3; 1863, p. 429; 1874, p. 364. Bháu Dájí, in the *Journ. Bom. Br. R. As. Soc.* article "Kalidasa," p. 31, and his revised translation of the inscription itself, *Journ. Bom. Br. R. As. Soc.* 1871, p. 59. General A. Cunningham in his *Archæological Report* for 1861-2, p. 92, gives a carefully corrected transcript of the original record, pl. XXX.

‡ *Journ. As. Soc. Beng.* 1874, p. 363, translation by Babu Rajendra Lála.

§ Under date 23rd April 1875, General Cunningham, in a private letter to Mr. Fergusson, reports the discovery of no less than four *new* inscriptions belonging to the Gupta period. "One of them is of Samudra Gupta, with the ṣlokas numbered in figures at the end. . . . A rock inscription of Chandra Gupta has the lines numbered in figures at the ends. A third inscription, dated S. 106, speaks of the Guptan maya, or Gupta family; and a fourth inscription is dated in S. 191."

|| Translation of Dr. Bhau Daji, *Journ. Bom. Br. R. As. Soc.*, vol. VII. p. 121.

century of *samvatsaras* (years) *plus* thirty *plus* seven" (in the "month of *Chaitra*") . . . on the "first day of the first lunation of the (first) month of the Ghíshma season," &c.

The concluding division of the inscription proclaims the completion of the undertaking, in the construction of a temple by Chakrapálita, when, "from the era of the Guptas (*Guptánán kála*) a century of years *plus* thirty-eight (having passed)."

Up to this time, I have been somewhat disposed to question the validity of the above interpretation, in respect to the use of the term *Gupta kála*. I have now had an opportunity of comparing Messrs. Westergaard and Jacob's facsimile, published in the *Journ. Bom. Br. R. As. Soc.* with Sir Le Grand Jacob's own eye-transcript in MS., and the improved version of the original, undertaken for Dr. Bhau Daji, by Pandurang Gopála Páḍhye. I can have no hesitation in accepting the latter as the most intelligent reproduction; it brings out into perfect form letters that were merely fragmentary before, it seldom conflicts with, but constantly improves what were previously chaotic signs and symbols in the copies of Messrs. Westergaard and Jacob.*

As regards the bearing of the term *Gupta kála* upon this and other dated inscriptions, while I am fully prepared to admit the figures 130–138 into the ordinary family system of reckoning, I am not so sure that the designation of *Gupta kála* in this instance, implies identity with Albírúní's understanding of the same term. I should rather connect it with the era then recognised and employed by the Gupta's, whatever its origin and derivation, in contrast to the *local* system of annual dates, which we find on the Sáh coins, and which clearly does not accord with the Eastern scheme of proximate usage.

No. 7. Translation of an Inscription on the Pillar at Eran in Bhopál. Dr. Fitzedward Hall's version.

"Triumphant is the four-armed divinity: omnipresent; of whom the broad waters of the four seas are the couch; cause of the continuance, origin, destruction, and the like, of the universe; whose ensign is Garuḍa. In the year 165 on the twelfth *day* of the light fortnight of the month of Áshádha† on the day of *Brihaspati*, and when Budha Gupta —ruling, with the genius of the regents of the quarters, over the interval, chosen land of the gods, between the Kálindí and the Narmadá . . . was king . . . a Brahman saint of the illustrious Maitráyaṇíya monarchs . . . the great king Mátṛivishṇu, a

* This copy, made for Dr. Bhau Dâjî, is reproduced as Plate XV. in this Report.

† It is necessary, in producing evidence for or against the ultimate import of these figures, to say that Professor Hall submitted the context of the passage embodying this date to Bápú Deva Ṣástrin, a Benáres mathematician, with a view to an opinion as to its concurrence with the Vikramáditya era or that of Ṣaka. The gist of the reply was, "it conforms to the era of Vikramáditya, and does not conform to that of Ṣáliváhana."—*Journ. As. Soc. Beng.* 1861, pp. 15–139. But with all respect for our Benáres calculator, we require to be told whether he has seen and met Colebrooke's objections to the effect that "the eclipses mentioned in the [later] grants do not appear reconcilable with their dates," and that "it seems difficult to account for this disagreement of the dates and eclipses in any other way than by impeaching the inscription, the authenticity of which there is not otherwise any reason to question."—(*Essays*, vol. II. p. 245.) See also (p. 357) for a possible explanation of the faulty results, in the introduction of "*Ráhu* as an eighth planet, and as the immediate cause of eclipses." Prof. Whitney, in his latest essay on "the Lunar Zodiac" (New York, 1874) ruthlessly exposes the imperfection of Indian astronomical knowledge and their methods of observation, which he climaxes by quoting their prediction of a *total* instead of a *partial* eclipse for February 6, 1860 (p. 368).

most devout worshipper of Bhagavat; who by the will of the Ordainer (Brahmá) acquired . . . the splendour of royalty . . and also of his younger brother Dhanyavishṇu, who does him obeisance," &c.*

We here take leave of Gupta dates and find ourselves in the presence of an inscription of Toramáṇa, who seems to have succeeded immediately to Budha Gupta's kingdom in central India. The importance of this monumental record will be better understood when we reach the numismatic sequence and obvious connexion between the two princes.

No. 8. Translation of an Inscription engraved on the neck of the Varáha image or Boar Incarnation at Eran.†

"Triumphant is the god who, in the likeness of a boar, lifted up the earth; who, by blows of his hard snout, tossed mountains aloft; the *upholding* pillar of that vast mansion, the three-fold world.

"In the first year that the auspicious Toramáṇa, sovereign of great kings, of extended fame and wide spread effulgence, is governing the earth; on the 10th day of Phálguna . . a Bráhman saint of the illustrious Maitráyaṇíya monarchs . . of the great king Mátṛivishṇu, who has departed to elysium, . . the younger brother Dhanyavishṇu, who did him due obeisance," &c.

No. 9. Inscription on the Porch of a Temple in the Fort of Gwalior.‡

"He who was celebrated as Ṣrí Toramáṇa . . full of talents innumerable, who subjugated the earth by truth, charity, conciliation, his army and the like. Unto him of the renowned race was born a son of unrivalled prowess named Pashupati, the lord of the earth, and the most distinguished of the Solar race . . in the fifteenth year of the prosperous reign of the remover of all suffering, the pre-eminent sovereign (lit. *Nṛipabṛisha*, 'the bull of kings')," &c.

Before taking leave of the subject of inscriptions, I wish to advert to a series of quasi-monumental documents for which, I think, too much value has been claimed. I mean the land and other royal grants or Ṣásanams engraved upon copper plates, and usually found in the possession of the families of the grantees.

I must confess that I have as little faith in these metallic title deeds, as the "Laws of Manu" seem to have extended to many of their earlier counterparts.§

---

* *Journ. As. Soc. Beng.* 1838, p. 634; 1861, p. 19.

† *Journ. As. Soc. Beng.* vol. VII. (1838), p. 633. Dr. Hall's revised rendering, above given, was published in the same Journal for 1861, p. 21.

‡ Bábu Rajendra Lála's version, *Journ. As. Soc. Beng.* 1861, p. 277.

§ Yájnavalkya, chap. II. sect. 240. "Whoever falsifies scales or a royal order."—Dr. Roer's Calcutta edition. Prof. Wilson translates "copper-plate grants by the head of the state."

I see that Mr. Burnell shares my distrust of this species of documents. He remarks: "Royal grants are by far the most important documents for historical purposes that exist in South India, such as they are; but they must be interpreted in the genealogical part with the greatest caution, especially those of the later dynasties, even if their authenticity be beyond suspicion. Unfortunately there is reason to believe that forgeries were common; for in the comparatively brief lists of crimes preserved in the Dharmaṣástra, the penalty of death is assigned for the forgeries of royal grants."—*Manu*, chap. IX. v. 232 (Haughton's translation, p. 324). *South Indian Palæography*, 1874, p. 76. See also Colebrooke's *Essays*, vol. II. pp. 236, 252–4, 264.

There is much of the air of manufacture even in those examples the genuineness of which we need not contest; but when we find formal repetition upon repetition, the same quotations of denunciatory texts recurring time after time, merging almost into the similitude of "a printed form of bequest," and we are told by impartial examiners of the present day that, in one case, the sign manual of the grantor proves to be in the writing of some centuries later than the forms of the letters of the text* to which he is asserted to have affixed his signature with his own hand (स्वहस्तो), we cannot divest ourselves of the suspicion that the dates may have been just as loosely manipulated as other portions of the documents themselves, especially when it is felt that the natural tendency, in such cases, would be to *ante-date*, with the view of giving meretricious age, authenticity and the semblance of perpetuity to the title.† It is true that this retention and continued use of the earlier form of character, for the body of the text, may merely imply the official recognition of a sort of black-letter style of writing in the local Patent Office, and that any intentional deception in the matter of the grant itself may have been foreign to the purpose of the engrossers; while, nevertheless, imposing or auspicious dates ‡ may have been *found*, or possibly old figures may have been copied mechanically with the standard phraseology from previous exemplars. I do not propose to enlarge upon the general question of the authenticity of these documents at the present moment, as they only contribute incidentally a side view to my leading subject; but it has become necessary to advert to the possible value of this species of evidence, as it has been occasionally put forward as a corrective of the true period of the Guptas, whose kingdom, in its western provinces, fell to the share of the Valabhís, who with their conterminous monarchies mainly supply the extant series of copper-plate grants, from whence these critical *test* dates are derived.

---

* This attestation or note at the end of the document is worthy of especial notice. The words are: "This is the own hand of Praṣánta-rága." . . . . "When the writing of this attestation is compared with the body of the grant, a very considerable difference is apparent. The general style of the whole, and the forms of many individual letters, present a much more modern appearance. Judging from the character of the writing alone by Prinsep's alphabets, it would seem to belong to a period at least three centuries later than the character and date of the grant itself."—Prof. J. Dowson, *Journ. R. As. Soc.* N. S. vol. I. p. 265.

† Prinsep had, from the first, felt a difficulty in reconciling the dates of the kings named in the Gujarát copper plates, remarking that "though there were six successions" (between the execution of the first and third Valabhí grants) "these must have been of less than the ordinary duration, for the minister who prepared the grant in Ṣrí Dharasena's reign was Skanda Bhaṭṭa; whereas the minister who prepared the present grant is named as Madana Híla, son of Skanda Bhaṭṭa. Thirty or forty years will, therefore, be the probable interval occupied by the reigns of all (these) princes." But it has been left for later decypherers to discover that the self-same Skanda Bhaṭṭa must have had a tenure of office lasting at least fifty-four years; and to confess that "our new grant shows that he held office under Guhasena also. If the second sign in the date of our grant is taken, with Prof. Bháṇḍárkar, for 50, the grant is dated in 256, consequently Skanda Bhaṭṭa must have been at least seventy years in office. It seems very improbable that a man should last so long."—Dr. Bühler, *Indian Antiquary*, June 1875, p. 174.

‡ I prefer, in this preliminary stage of the inquiry, to quote the unprejudiced and casually-pronounced opinions of others who have had to comment, directly or indirectly, on the measure of reliance that can be placed upon the "time tables" of the western copper plates. General Cunningham, without contesting the real data these documents might supply, expresses himself as follows in regard to Dr. Bhau Daji's Brief Survey of Indian Chronology (*Journ. Bom. Br. R. As. Soc.* vol. VIII. p. 236), in order "to note the curious error in what he calls a *correct* genealogical table of the Balabhi kings supported by dates from copper plates. In this genealogy I notice that Dhruvasena, who is dated in 310, is followed by *six* generations, all of which are made to pass away by 346, so that *seven generations*, including Dhruvasena, or six without him, are born, marry, and die in thirty-six years, which allows exactly six years to each generation."—Cunningham's *Arch. Report*, I. xxxiv.

In conclusion, I wish it to be distinctly understood that my objections do not extend to the good faith of royal grants or private endowments for religious purposes, when the texts, embodying the terms of the benefaction, are formally inscribed *on stone* in or near the building, cave, or other monument in whose cause the grant is made. In these cases there must have been a dedicatory formality and an abiding publicity which forbids all idea of deception, and hence this class of documents, as will be seen hereafter, may be welcomed as among the most trustworthy data within our reach.

b.—Written History.

We have now to collect the passages wherein chance mention of the Guptas is to be found in works compiled in India. Written history in its proper sense has rarely been attempted in that land, and the materials now available are confined to the pseudo-prophecies of the Puráṇas, the chance allusions to imperial changes which find a place in the local history of the valley of Kashmír, and the critical investigations of Albírúní, which are only raised above tradition by his elaborate exposition of dates and eras, which elucidate the rise and fall of so many dynastic rulers of Hind.

The Vishṇu-Puráṇa.

"In Magadha, a sovereign named Viṣwasphaṭika will establish other tribes: he will extirpate the Kshattriya (or martial) race, and elevate fishermen (Kaivarta), barbarians (Yadus and Pulindás), and Brahmans (and other castes) to power." "The nine Nágas will reign in Padmávatí, Kántipurí and Mathurá; and the Guptas of Magadha along the Ganges to Prayága." The Váyu-Puráṇa has another series analogous to that of the (Vishṇu-Puráṇa) text. "The nine Náka kings will possess the city Champávatí; and the seven Nágas (?), the pleasant city of Mathurá. Princes of the Gupta race will possess all these countries, the banks of the Ganges to Prayága, and Sáketa, and Mágadhá (the Magadhas)." Professor Wilson adds, "This account is the most explicit, and probably the most accurate of all. The Nákas were Rájas of Bhagulpúr; the Nágas of Mathurá*; and the intermediate countries along the Ganges were governed by the Guptas (or Rájas of the Vaiṣya caste).†

The Rája Tarangini.

The Rája Tarangini, which has more pretensions to systematic history than most works of its class, is a compilation from various authorities, arranged by Kalhaṇa Paṇḍit, in Ṣaka 1070=A.D. 1148.

Though taking an avowedly provincial view of the annals of Kashmír, it contributes incidentally several suggestive combinations with the larger margin of Indian

---

* *Journ. As. Soc. Beng.* 1865, pp. 116, 117. See also *Journ. As. Soc. Beng.* 1837, pp. 10, 16, 17; and Wilford, *Asiatic Researches*, vol. IX. pp. 114, 115. Wilford says, "then came a dynasty of nine kings, called the nine Nágás, or Nákás. These were an obscure tribe, called for that reason, *Gupta-vansas*: there were nine families of them, who ruled independent of each other, over various districts in Anuganjam; such as Padmávati [Champávatí], Kántipurí, Magadha, Prayága, Saketa, and Benares."

† The Vishṇu-Puráṇa expressly says, "Gupta and Dása are best fitted for the names of Vaiṣyas and Śúdras." Wilson's *Vishṇu-Puráṇa*, edited by Dr. Fitzedward Hall, vol. IV. p. 218; Quarto edit., Oriental Translation Fund, book IV., cap. xxiv. p. 479.

imperial politics. It gives us, in the most complete form we are able to cite, a notice of the dominant Scythic brotherhood, which extended its sway to Mathurá on the one side, and to Bháwalpúr on the other, before the Gupta rule; regarding which, if the chronicle is wholly silent, it furnishes suggestive indications of the extinction of their power, in the accession of a Toramáṇa, should this joint king of the Kashmír Chronicle eventually prove to be identical with the monarch named in the inscriptions at Eran and Gwálior given in abstract, pp. 5–6 ante.

After enumerating the reigns of (1) Aṣoka, (2) Jaloka (s. f.), and (3) Dámodhara, the chronicle continues :—

"Dámodhara was succeeded by three princes who divided the country, and severally founded capital cities named after themselves. These princes were called Hushka, Jushka, and Kanishka,* of Turushka or Tatar extraction. . . . They are considered synchronous, but may possibly be all that are preserved of some series of Tatar princes who, it is very likely, at various periods, established themselves in Kashmír."†

"Ṣreshṭasena also called Pravarasena reigned 30 years and left his kingdom to his two sons Hiraṇya and Toramáṇa; the former holding the superior station of the *Sámrájya*, and the latter that of the *Yauvarájya*, or being respectively Emperor and Cæsar, a division of power of considerable antiquity amongst the Hindus. . . . . The latter having proceeded to strike coins (*dínárs*) in his own name, the elder brother (the *Sámrája*) took offence at the measure, and deposed the *Yuvarája* and kept him in close confinement. . . . . Toramáṇa died in captivity. The ruler of Ujain at that time was Ṣríman Harsha Vikramáditya, who after expelling the Mlechchhas and destroying the Ṣakas, had established his power and influence throughout India. In his train was a Brahman named Mátṛi-gupta to whom he was much attached; upon hearing of the vacant situation of the Kashmír throne, he recommended Mátṛi-gupta for election, who was accepted by the nobles as their king."

Albírúní.

A marked contrast will be detected between the vague utterances and confined purpose of the Hindu Pandit and the critical efforts at precision and comprehensive range of inquiry of the Muslim mathemetician,‡ trained in the old *nidus* of Aryanism,

---

* Abulfazl says "brothers." Gladwin's Translation, ii. 171.

General Cunningham considers that he has succeeded in identifying all the three capitals the sites of which are placed within the limits of the valley of Kashmír, *i.e.*,

"*Kanishka-pura* (Kanikhpur) hod. Kámpur, is 10 miles S. of Sirinagar, known as Kámpur Sarai.

"*Hushka-pura*, the Hu-se-kia-lo of Hiuen Thsang—the Ushkar of Albírúní—now surviving in the village of *Uskara*, 2 miles S.E. of Baráhmula.

"*Jushka-pura* is identified by the Brahmans with Zukru or Zukur, a considerable village 4 miles N. of the capital, the *Schecroh* of Troyer and Wilson."—*Ancient Geography of India*, London, 1871, p. 99.

† Prof. H. H. Wilson, "An Essay on the Hindu History of Kashmír," *Asiatic Researches*, vol. XV. p. 23. See also Troyer's Histoire des Rois du Kachmir, vol. II. p. 19. See also Hiouen-Thsang, Paris, 1858, vol. II. pp. 42, 106, &c.

‡ In the proper order of dates Albírúní precedes the author of the *Rája Taranginí*. I have placed him last in the present résumé as giving the fullest summary of dates and events, and as more directly associated with tradition, which singularly supports some of his most contested statements.

who came in the suite of the great Mahmúd of Ghazní,* not to participate in the devastating plunder of the conqueror, but to investigate the science and learning of the land, a task for which he was eminently fitted by his previous studies, and into which he entered with a philosophical earnestness altogether foreign to the rough associations around him. The result, confessedly imperfect, has been embodied in his Táríkh-i-Hind, from which the following epitome of the serial dates culminating in the Gupta era has been extracted.

" On emploie ordinairement les ères de Sri-Harcha, de Vikramâditya, de Saca, de Ballaba, et des Gouptas. . . L'ère de Vikramâditya est employée dans les provinces méridionales et occidentales de l'Inde. . . L'ère de Saca, nommée par les Indiens 'Saca-kâla,' est postérieure à celle de Vikramâditya de 135 ans. Saca est le nom d'un prince qui a régné sur les contrées situées entre l'Indus et la mer. Sa résidence était placée

* Abú Ríhán *Muhammad bin Ahmad* al Bírúní *al Khwárizmí* was born about A.H. 360, A.D. 970–1. He was an astronomer, geometrician, historian, and logician, under which latter claim he obtained the sobriquet of "*Muhakkik*" or "the exact," on account of the rigorous precision of his deductions. Abú-l Fazl Baihakí, who lived about half a century after Al Bírúní, says, "*Bú Ríhán* was beyond comparison superior to every man of his time in the art of composition, in scholar-like accomplishments, and in knowledge of geometry and philosophy. He had, moreover, a most rigid regard for truth ;" and Rashídu-d dín, in referring to the great writer from whom he has borrowed so much, says, "The Master *Abú Ríhán* al Bírúní excelled all his contemporaries in the sciences of philosophy, mathematics, and geometry. He entered the service of Mahmúd bin Subuktigín, and in the course of his service he spent a long time in Hindustan, and learned the language of the country. Several of the provinces of India were visited by him. He was on friendly terms with many of the great and noble of that country, and so acquired an intimate knowledge of their books of philosophy, religion, and belief. The best and most excellent of all their books upon the arts and sciences is one resembling the work of Shaikh Raís Abú 'Alí ibn Siná (*Avicenna*). It is called Bátakal, or in Arabic Bátajal ; this book he translated into Arabic. From this work also he extracted a great deal which he made use of in his Kánún-i Mas'údi, a work upon mathematics and geometry, named after the Sultán Mas'úd. All that the sages of India have said about numbers, ages, and eras (*tawáríkh*), has been exactly given by *Abú Ríhán* in his translation of the Bátakal. He was indebted to the Sultán of Khwárizm for the opportunity of visiting India, for he was appointed by him to accompany the embassies which he sent to Mahmúd of Ghazni. Al Farábí and Abú-l Khair joined one of these embassies, but the famous *Avicenna*, who was invited to accompany them, refused to go, being, as it is hinted, averse to enter into controversy with Abú Ríhán, with whom he differed on many points of science, and whose logical powers he feared to encounter. On the invitation of Mahmúd, *Abú Ríhán* entered into his service, an invitation which *Avicenna* declined. It was in the suite of Mahmúd and of his son Mas'úd that *Abú Ríhán* travelled into India and he is reported to have staid forty years there. He died in A.H. 430, A.D. 1038–9. He wrote many works, and is said to have executed several translations from the Greek, and epitomised the Almagest of Ptolemy. His works are stated to have exceeded a camel-load, insomuch that it was supposed by devout Muhammadans that he received divine aid in his compositions. Those most spoken of are astronomical tables, a treatise on precious stones, one on Materia Medica, an introduction to astrology, a treatise on chronology, and the famous Kánúni-Mas'údí, an astronomical and geographical work frequently cited by Abú-l Fidá, especially in his tables of latitudes and longitudes." (Sir H. Elliot's Historians of India.) Sir H. Rawlinson, in a late number of the "Quarterly Review," observes : "*Abú Ríhán* was the only early Arab writer who investigated the antiquities of the east in a true spirit of historical criticism," and he proceeds to give some examples of his knowledge of ancient technical chronology which are of the highest importance in establishing the early civilization of the Aryan race. Abú Ríhán declares that "the solar calendar of his native province, Khwárizm, was the most perfect scheme for measuring time with which he was acquainted, and it was maintained by the astronomers of that country, that both the solar and the lunar Zodiacs had originated with them ; the divisions of the signs in their systems being far more regular than those adopted by the Greeks or Arabs. Another statement of *Abú Ríhán's* asserts that the Khwárizmians dated originally from an epoch anterior by 980 years to the era of the Seleucidæ (equal to B.C. 1304), a date which agrees pretty accurately with the period assigned by our best scholars to the invention of the Jyotisha or Indian calendar." Though I am bound to add that the authenticity of the latter test is by no means unquestioned.

au centre de l'empire, dans la contrée nommée Aryavartha. Les Indiens le font naître dans une classe autre que celle des Sakya; quelques-uns prétendent qu'il était Soudra et originaire de la ville de Mansoura; il y en a même qui disent qu'il n'était pas de race indienne, et qu'il tirait son origine des régions occidentales. Les peuples eurent beaucoup à souffrir de son despotisme, jusqu'à ce qu'il leur vint du secours de l'Orient. Vikramáditya marcha contre lui, mit son armée en déroute, et le tua sur le territoire de Korour, situé entre Moultan et le château de Louny. Cette époque devint célèbre, à cause de la joie que les peuples ressentirent de la mort de Saca, et on la choisit pour ère principalement chez les astronomes.

"Ballaba, qui a donné aussi son nom à une ère, était prince de la ville de Ballaba, au midi de Anhalouara, à environ trente *yodjanas* de distance. L'ère de Ballaba est postérieure à celle de Saca de 241 ans. Pour s'en servir, on pose l'ère de Saca, et l'on en ôte à la fois le cube de 6 (216) et le carré de 5 (25). Ce qui reste est l'ère de Ballaba. Il sera question de cette ère en son lieu. Quant au Goupta-kála (ère des Gouptas), on entend par le mot *goupta* des gens qui, dit-on, étaient méchants et puissants; et l'ère qui porte leur nom est l'époque de leur extermination. Apparemment, Ballaba suivit immédiatement les Gouptas; car l'ère des Gouptas commence aussi l'an 241 de l'ère de Saca. L'ère des astronomes commence l'an 587 de l'ère de Saca. C'est à cette ère qu'ont été rapportées les tables Kanda Khátaka, de Brahma goupta. Cet ouvrage porte chez nous le titre de *Arkand.* D'après cela, en s'en tenant à l'an 400 de l'ère de Yezderdjed, on se trouve sous l'année 1488 de l'ère de Sri-Harscha, l'an 1088 de l'ère de Vikramáditya, l'an 953 de l'ère de Saca, l'an 712 de l'ère de Ballaba et celle des Gouptas. . . .

"Déjà je me suis excusé sur l'imperfection de ce qui est dit ici, et j'ai averti que les résultats que je présente offraient quelque incertitude, vu les nombres qui excèdent celui de cent."*—*Journal Asiatique,* 4me série, tom. iv. (1844).

M. Reinaud's translation here quoted was based upon a confessedly imperfect copy of the then unique but faulty Constantinople MS. of the Táríkh-i-Hind. It has frequently been called in question by those Indian commentators to whom its data came as a revelation from within. As I had to a certain extent accepted the value and importance of the information it conveyed, I sought the earliest opportunity of confirming or correcting its terms by the text of the new and more perfect manuscript of M. Schefer, which has been entrusted to Professor Sachau to aid his grand undertaking of a corpus of the works of Albírúní; the most important sections of which are about to be published under the joint auspices of the London Oriental Translation Fund and the German Text Society.

---

* Albírúní, in another part of his work, attributes many of the complications and obscurities imported into Indian texts, to the prevailing system of reducing everything into verse, for the sake of the obvious facility of learning by heart, so often to the entire detriment of the sense of the original; he adds, "J'ai reconnu, à mes dépens, l'inconvénient de cet usage."—Reinaud Mem. sur l'Inde, p. 334. Perhaps one of the most instructive expositions of the gradations of the process, under which the Indian art of memory was forced and matured, is to be found in Professor Haug's paper, presented to the Oriental Congress of London in 1874, from which I take the following extracts :—

"The *Veda* is the only sacred code that has been handed down to posterity solely by oral tradition, which has remained, even up to the present day, the only legitimate way of transmitting the ancient divine

M. Sachau has kindly sent me the subjoined list of variants from M. Reinaud's printed Arabic text,* but naturally prefers to await a final revision of the whole work, a larger acquaintance with Albîrûnî's style, and a consideration of the combined difficulty of this portion of the text, with the intricacies of Indian mathematical calculations before committing himself to any revised translation, such as I desired to have substituted for the French version now quoted."

c.—Tradition.

There remains, under this section of our inquiry, the single avowed dole of *tradition* the odd corners of the land have preserved intact, to support much that was previously

---

knowledge to the future generations of Brahmans. The wonderful state of correctness in which the ancient Vedic texts have reached our time may well excite our admiration, principally, if we bear in mind, that this is exclusively owing to oral teaching, and not to the use of MSS. Although the Brahmans are at present in the possession of MSS. of their sacred books, they are never used for instruction. The Brahman boy has to acquire all knowledge of sacred texts from the mouth of a competent and properly qualified teacher, but never from a MS. For according to Brahmanical notions, which are still current, that *Veda* only which is in the mouth of the Brahmans is the true *Veda ;* all knowledge of it that has been acquired from MSS. is no longer regarded as *Veda.* The use of them is only permitted in the way of assisting the memory, after the oral instruction has been completed. In former times the aid afforded by MSS. could be more readily dispensed with, since oral instruction took about thirty years, whereas it is now reduced to about half the time. In order to prevent those who had learnt the *Veda* from the mouth of the teacher from ever forgetting what they had committed to memory, it was made incumbent on them to communicate before their death their sacred knowledge to qualified persons. By such means it has been really brought about that the Vedic texts, that is, the *Mantras, Bráhmaṇas, Upanishads,* and *Vedángas,* rest so firmly in the heads of the professional Vedics, the so-called *Bhaṭṭas,* that if all the MSS. should be collected and destroyed, they could be restored in the very words, even to each single letter and accent, from memory, as I was often assured by trustworthy Brahmans during my six years' stay in the *Mahratta* country. Hence one might justly attribute to texts obtained from a body of renowed Vedics, both in the *Sañhitá* and *Pada* forms, at least the same degree of accuracy and authority which is ascribed to an edition prepared from a number of the best MSS. ; for all really good MSS. have not been copied by the *Bhaṭṭas* from others, but written from memory ; errors which may be detected in MSS. are generally not corrected by consulting other copies, but on the authority of the living tradition, viz., one of the *Bhaṭṭas,* since any Vedic text which is written is never looked upon with the same degree of confidence that is attached to oral tradition. * * * I once had occasion to converse with a large number of *Bhaṭṭas,* who are the legitimate preservers of Vedic texts ; they told me, to my surprise, that the understanding of the texts they were in the habit of reciting was regarded as perfectly useless, and was consequently wholly disregarded. They learn the *Vedas* by heart for practical purposes, only to recite them at the sacrifices, or before private individuals of the Brahman caste who may wish to hear them for their welfare.

"Although this opinion seems to have prevailed with the professional reciters among the Brahmans, it was fortunately not shared by the more intelligent and inquisitive members of their caste, who looked upon the *Bhaṭṭas* as a kind of beasts of burden, carrying loads without knowing their nature.

*	Reinaud's text.	Schefer (MS. fol. 108–9).		Reinaud's text.	Schefer (MS. fol. 108–9).
p. 128, l. 5.	حمن	جمن	p. 129, l. 14.	والامتداد	ولامتداد
p. 128, l. 6.	حمن	جمن	p. 129, l. 14.	زمن	زمر
p. 128, l. 11.	السابقة	السابعة	p. 130, l. 1.	فكان	فكانوا
p. 128, l. 16.	محلة	بجلة	p. 130, l. 2.	وكانّ بلب	وبلب
p. 128, l. 20.	جندرينه	جنّدريين or بيز	p. 130, l. 8.	پنج	سح
p. 129, l. 2.	مجزبا	معزبا	p. 130, l. 8.	۹٢۴	٥٢۴
p. 129, l. 8.	شوددا	شودرا	p. 130, l. 9.	۱۹	٢٥

irreconcileable in the statements of Albírúní. The tradition may be imperfect* as such old-world tales are liable to become, but there is an instructive confirmation of one obscure portion of the earlier history given by the Muhammadan inquirer, and a clear explanation of the causes of the local transfer of power, combined with an important reference to the conventional Imperial delegation of authority to a son, as well as an indication of the length of the reigns of two kings, to be found nowhere else; and to complete the tale, we trace in its details a fully reasonable accord with the more precise data furnished independently by inscriptions and coins.

"The bards relate that Váḷá Rájá, son of Váḷá Warsingji, reigned in Junágaḍh and Vanthalí. . . . Ráma Rájá was of the Váḷá race. It is said in Sauráshṭra that, previous to the rise of the kingdom of Junágaḍh-Vanthalí, Valabhinagar was the capital of Gujarát. The rise of Valabhi is thus told by the bards. 'The Gupta kings reigned between the Ganges and Jamná rivers. One of these kings sent his son Kumára-pál Gupta to conquer Sauráshṭra, and placed his viceroy Chakrapáni, son of Prándat, one of his Amírs, to reign as provincial governor in the city of Wámanasthalí (the modern Wanthali). Kumára-pál now returned to his father's kingdom. His father reigned twenty-three years after the conquest of Sauráshṭra and then died, and Kumára-pála ascended the throne. Kumára-pál Gupta reigned twenty years and then died, and was succeeded by Skanda Gupta, but this king was of weak intellect. His *senápati*, Bhaṭṭaraka, who was of the Gehlotí race, taking a strong army, came into Sauráshṭra, and made his rule firm there. Two years after this Skanda Gupta died. The *senápati* now assumed the title of King of Sauráshṭra, and, having placed a governor at Wámanasthalí, founded the city of Valabhinagar. At this time the Gupta race were dethroned by foreign invaders."†

* Professor Báṇḍarkar has criticised certain items of this tradition in the following terms:—

"But the tradition itself, though interesting as giving the truth generally, cannot be considered to be true in the particulars. For, in the first place, it makes Chakrapáṇi the son of Prándat, who is certainly the Chakrapáḷita son of Parṇadatta of the Junágaḍh inscription (*Journ. Bom. Br. R. As. Soc.* vol. VII. pp. 122, 123, *supra* p. 4), viceroy of the father of Kumára Gupta, and grandfather of Skanda Gupta, while the inscription represents Parṇadatta as Skanda Gupta's viceroy, and Chakrapálita as governor of a certain town, appointed to that place by his own father. Again, Skanda Gupta is represented as a weak king in the tradition; while his inscriptions, magniloquent though they are, do show that he must have been a powerful monarch. Lastly, Bhaṭárka is mentioned as having assumed the title of King, while the Valabhí copper plates speak of him as Senápati, and represent Droṇa Sinha, his second son, to have first assumed that title. (*Journ. As. Soc. Bengal*, vol. IV., Mr. Wathen and an unpublished grant of Guhasena). The tradition, therefore, is not entitled to any reliance as regards the particulars. It simply gives us what was known before, that the Valabhís succeeded the Guptas."—*Indian Antiquary*, vol. III. (1874), p. 303.

† Major J. W. Watson, Legends of Junágaḍh, *Indian Antiquary*, (Nov. 1873,) vol. II., p. 312.

d.—Coins.

As fitly introductory to the Gupta gold coinage, I prefix a specimen prototype in the rare and little known coins of the Indo-Scythian king *Vásudeva*, whose name or title figures so prominently in the Mathurá inscriptions.

As the general range of the dates and localities of the Indo-Scythian inscriptions are calculated to throw important light upon the history of the period, and have a special bearing upon the distribution of the contemporary Baktrian and Indian Páli alphabets, I annex a résumé of these documents lately prepared for my publication on "Ancient Indian Weights."*

Indo-Scythian Inscriptions (in the Indo-Páli Alphabet).

At Mathurá.—Kanishka. *Mahárája Kanishka.* *Samvat* 9.

Huvishka. *Mahárája* Devaputra *Huvishka.* Hemanta, *S.* 39.

Mahárája Rájatirája Devaputra *Huvishka.* Grishma, *S.* 47.

Mahárája Huvishka. Hemanta, *S.* 48.

Vásudeva. *Mahárája Rájátirája* Devaputra *Vásu(deva).* Varsha, *S.* 44.

Mahárája Vásudeva. Grishma, *S.* 83.

Mahárája Rájatirája, Sháhi, *Vásudeva.* Hemanta, *S.* 87.

Rája Vásudeva. Varsha, *S.* 98.

Indo-Scythian Inscriptions (in the Baktrian-Páli Alphabet).

In other localities.—Bháwalpúr. *Maharaja Rajadiraja* Devaputra *Kanishka.* Samvat 11, on the 28th of the (Greek) month of Dæsius.†

Manikyála Tope. *Maharaja Kaneshka*, Gushana *vaṣa samvardhaka.* "Increaser of the dominion of the Gushans" (Kushans). *Samvat* 18.

Wardak Vase. *Maharaja rajatiraja Huveshka.* *Samvat* 51, 15th of Artemisius.

In addition to these Baktrian-Páli inscriptions, we have a record in the same alphabet, of a king called Moga (Moa?), on a copper plate from Taxila, wherein the *Satrap Liako Kusuluko* (Kozola?) speaks of the 78th year of the "great king, the great *Moga*," on the 5th of the month of Panæmus; and an inscription from Takht-i-Bahi of King Gondophares, dated in his 26th year, with a corresponding entry of the month of Vaiṣákh, Samvat 103.‡

---

* "Ancient Indian Weights." The introductory chapter of Marsden's *Numismata Orientalia*, Trübner, 1874.

† The opening line of the Zeda inscription of Samvat 11, with the Indian month *of Ashádha*, can only be doubtfully associated with the two lines of small writing below it, in which the name of Kanishka is found. Cunningham's *Arch. Rep.* vol. V. p. 57.

‡ *Journ. R. As. Soc.* vol. VII. N. S. p. 377; Cunningham, *Arch. Rep.* vol. V. p. 59.

It would contribute very material aid towards the reconstruction of the general chronology of India if we could determine the era to which these inscription dates refer; it is clear that many of them are mere regnal dates, but as some of them run up as high as 98, this alone puts them beyond any such confined system of reckoning, and even outside the probable duration of the combined reigns of the three brothers, "Hushka, Jushka and Kaniskka" of the Kashmír chronicles.

The next point we have to consider is the nature of the inscriptions themselves, as a rule they are not royal manifestoes, but records of the piety, in gifts or endowments, of private individuals, and as such would primarily refer to some well established and generally recognised era. What was that era? Vikramáditya (57 B.C.) would place the documents too early; Ṣaka (79 A.D.*) too late. I have recently suggested the claims of the Seleucidan era (1st September, B.C. 312), allowing for the omission of the current figure for *hundreds*, which is now discovered to have been the practice adopted by the Baktrian Greeks.

As the simplest way of stating my views, under the latter aspect, I quote in its integrity a letter I lately addressed to "*The Academy*," which has already attracted much attention among Numismatists.†

"*Baktrian Coins and Indian Dates.*

"December 16, 1874.

"Those of your readers who concern themselves with the vexed question of Indian dates may be interested to learn that evidence of some importance, in that direction, has recently been obtained from the coins of the Baktrian Greeks. Since Bayer's premature attempt to interpret a Mint-monogram on a piece of Eukratides as 108,‡ Numismatists have not lost sight of the possible discrimination of dates as opposed to Mint-marks on the surfaces of these issues.§

"In 1858 I published, in my edition of Prinsep's *Essays on Indian Antiquities*, a notice of the detached letters **OΓ** as occurring on a coin of Eukratides (No. 3, p. 184, vol. II.) and **ΠΓ** as found on the money of Heliokles (No. 1, p. 182), which letters would severally represent the figures 73 and 83; but these numbers were apparently too low to afford any satisfactory elucidation in their application as dynastic dates.

"On a chance visit to the British Museum, a short time ago, Mr. Percy Gardner was so obliging as to show me all the latest acquisitions of Baktrian coins, and among them a specimen of Heliokles with the full triliteral date, after the manner of the Syrian mints, of **PΠΓ** or 183,‖ which, when tested by the Seleucidan era (311–183), brings his reign under the convenient date of B.C. 128, and authorises us to use the abbreviated figures, under the same terms, as **OΓ**=73 for 173 Sel.=138 B.C. for Eukratides, and

* Monday, 14th March, A.D. 78, Julian style.

† *Num. Chron.* 1875, p. 5; Agra Archæological Society, Annual Meeting, 1875.

‡ *Hist. Reg. Graecorum Bactriani.* St. Petersburg, 1738, p. 44.

§ H. H. Wilson, *Ariana Antiqua*, pp. 235, 238. General A. Cunningham, *Numismatic Chronicle*, vol. IX. N. S. p. 230.

‖ The *unique* coin of Plato lately purchased by the British Museum, which is closely associated in its obverse device with the money of Eukratides, is also dated, apparently, **PMZ** = 147 Sel., or 164 B.C. A full description, with an illustrative woodcut of this coin, has since been published by Mr. Vaux in the *Numismatic Chronicle* for 1875, p. 6.

the repeated ΠΓ=83 for 183 Sel.=128 for Heliokles, a date which is further supported by the appearance of the exceptionally combined *open* monogram |Ā| (ΠA), or 81 for 181=130 B.C. on his other pieces.

"In addition to the value of these data as fixing definitively, though within fairly anticipated limits, the epochs of these prominent Baktrian kings, the conventional use of the abbreviated definition introduces us at once to local customs, to which the Greeks so readily lent themselves, in their adoption of the method of reckoning by the Indian *Loka Kála*,* which simplified the expression of dates, as we do now, in the civilised year of our Lord, when we write 74 for 1874.

"The domestication of the Seleucidan era and its incorporation of Indian methods of calculation, leads on to the consideration of how long this exotic system of computation maintained its ground in Upper India, and how much influence it exerted upon the chronological records of succeeding dynasties. I have long been under the impression that this influence was more widespread and abiding than my fellow antiquarians have been ready to admit,† but I am now prepared to carry my inferences into newer channels, and to suggest, as a commencement, that the Indo-Scythian 'Kanishka' kings continued to use the Seleucidan era, even as they retained the minor sub-divisions of the Greek months which formed an essential part of its system; and under this view to propose that we should treat the entire range of dates of the 'Hushka, Jushka, and Kanishka' *family* of the Rája Taranginí,‡ which their inscriptions expand from ix. to xcviii.§, as pertaining to the fourth century of the Seleucidan era, an arrangement which will bring them into concert with our reckoning from 2 B.C. to 87 A.D. A scheme which would moreover provide for their full possession of power up to the *crucial* 'Ṣaka' date of 78–79 A.D., and allow for the continuance of certain local reigns as claimed by their subordinate public epigraphs.

"The Ṣaka era, with its Indian months as recorded in the Gupta inscriptions,‖ belongs to a new order of things, but this much may be added in conclusion, that the earliest epigraph of Chandra Gupta, the fifth of that race, dated in 82 Ṣaka, or 161 A.D., leaves a satisfactory margin for the heroic efforts and successful conquests of the second Vikramáditya (of Albírúní's legends) and his immediate successors."

I have no wish to press these suggestions for more than they are worth, or to precipitate a decision in their favour; but in addition to the incorporation of the Macedonian months in the Baktrian-Páli inscriptions, which clearly, in their higher numbers, follow an identical era with the Mathurá dedicatory epigraphs couched in the Indian Páli alphabet, there are many other evidences of the spread and continued use

---

* Albírúní, writing in India in 1031 A.D., tells us, "Le vulgaire, dans l'Inde, compte par siècles, et les siècles se placent l'un après l'autre. On appelle cela le Samvatsara du cent. Quand un cent est écoulé, on le laisse et l'on en commence un autre. On appelle cela Loka-kála, c'est-à-dire comput du peuple."—(Reinaud's Translation, *Fragments Arabes*, Paris, 1845.)

† *Journ. R. As. Soc.* vol. XII. p. 41; *Journ. As. Soc. Beng.* 1855, p. 565, and 1872, p. 175; Prinsep's *Essays*, vol. II. p. 86; *Journal Asiatique*, 1863, p. 388.

‡ P. 10, *supra.*

§ *Journ. R. As. Soc.* vol. V. N.S. p. 122. "Ancient Indian Weights," 1874, p. 46. General Cunningham's *Arch. Rep.* vol. III. p. 29. (Reproduced above, p. 16.)

‖ Prinsep's *Essays*, vol. I. p. 231 *et seq.*

of the Seleucidan system of dating,* which would have tended to commend it to the less enlightened occupying Scythians who succeeded to outlying sections of the dominions of the Baktrian Greeks in India.

The Indo-Scythian inscriptions extant at Mathurá are not dated in *months*, but in the old triple seasons, *Grishma*, *Varsha*, and *Hemanta*, like so many of the ancient writings in the caves of Western India,† and it is a suggestive fact, as bearing upon the omission or non-specification of the *hundreds*, that none of the Indo-Scythian inscriptions at Mathurá run into three figures: they approach closely but do not touch the *100*. And the first inscription, *in situ*, of *later* date, or 135 of some undefined *Samvat*, presents us with the earliest specimen among these records of a fully developed *Hindu* month (*Pushya*).‡

Since the publication of my letter of the 15th December 1874 Albírúní's account of the method of dating, in the *Lokakála*, by the omission of the *even* hundreds, has been opportunely confirmed by the discovery that the inhabitants of Kashmír follow this system of computation in all its integrity to the present day.§

I am well aware that Menander had so far departed from the traditional Indo-Greek abbreviated dates, as to confine himself on his coins to *regnal* years, inasmuch as I am able to cite from his extant money the dates A 1, B 2, Γ 3, Δ 4, E 5, H 8; but this no more proves the general surrender of the consecutive eral system of dating than the Mathurá regnal dates establish the rule in the mixed instances above adverted to.

I can also quote a newly discovered Parthian era, commencing in 248 B.C.‖ which viewing its now ascertained employment in the Cuneiform documents of the

---

* Since proposing the above identifications, I have examined all the Baktrian coins within reach to seek for new examples of these abbreviated dates, but without success. I am able, however, to revert to two very curious contributions in the same line from the coins of Apollodotus, in the letters Ξ = 60 and ΞE = 65, published by me some years ago in Prinsep's *Essays*, vol. II. p. 188, and in the *Numismatic Chronicle*, vol. XIX. p. 22 (*Monograms*, p. 66). Under the system of the omission of the hundreds, these dates would correspond with B.C. 151 and 146—a period which would not be at all inappropriate for this king, who has been variously placed by Lassen at 160 B.C., by Wilson at 110 B.C., and by Cunningham at 165 B.C. One coincidence in connexion with these two Greek *letter*-dates is that they are in both cases either preceded or succeeded by the letters NO in a similar position at the foot of the device on the reverse, which may possibly stand for the *initial* letters of *νόμος* "usage, custom," &c., or some of its derivative forms, though this is avowedly a mere conjecture open to further investigation.

† Cunningham's *Arch. Report*, vol. p. III. 36; *Journ. R. As. Soc.* vol. V. p. 190, and the Cave Inscriptions, in the *Journ. Bom. Br. R. As. Soc.* See also *Hiuen Thsang*, vol. II. p. 63; and Elliot's *Glossary*, vol. II. p. 47.

‡ This can by no possibility be made into a Vikramáditya date; it is more than a question if it can even refer to Ṣaka. Similarly, in regard to these dates, I am altogether undisturbed by the *Hindu* month in the Gondophares inscription, p. 30 *ante*; in short, whenever we pass *the hundred* we lose Seleucidan *months*, though it would be unwise to propound any absolute law on the subject with our present scanty materials.

§ This second inscription ends with the words *Ṣaka Kála* gatávdah 726—that is, "Ṣáka Kál years elapsed 726," equivalent to A.D. 804, which is therefore the date of the temple. This date also corresponds with the year 80 of the local cycle, which is the *Lok-kál* of Kashmír or cycle of 2,700 years, counted by centuries named after the 27 *nakshatras*, or lunar mansions. The reckoning, therefore, never goes beyond 100 years, and as each century begins in the 25th year of the Christian century, the 80th year of the local cycle is equivalent to the 4th year of the Christian century. General Cunningham, *Arch. Rep.* 1875, vol. V. p. 181. See also Dr. Bühler's *Report*, quoted in the *Athenæum* of the 20th Nov. 1875.

‖ *Assyrian Discoveries*, by George Smith. London, 1875, p. 389. From the time of the Parthian conquest it appears that the tablets were dated according to the Parthian style. There has always been a doubt as to the date of this revolt, and consequently of the Parthian monarchy, as the classical authorities have left no evidence as to the exact date of the rise of the Parthian power. I, however, obtained three Parthian tablets from Babylon; two of them contained double dates, one of which, being found perfect, supplied the required evidence, as it was

period, and obvious official preference may have secured a larger range of acceptance than could otherwise have been conjectured, and may thus, in its associate extension with the power of the race, arrogate some claim to rule and regulate our obscure Indo-Scythian dates. Testing the Mathurá figures by this system with its third century commencing in 48 B.C., we have another possible approximation towards the solution of this great enigma.

The comparative estimates by the four methods of computation, stand roughly as follows :—

Vikramáditya - - - -	B.C. 48 to A.D. 41.
Ṣaka - - - - -	A.D. 88 to A.D. 177.
Seleucidan - - - -	B.C. 2 to A.D. 87.
Parthian - - - -	B.C. 39 to A.D. 50.

VÁSUDEVA.

No. I✱.* Gold.

Trésor de Numismatique, Pl. LXXX. figs. 10, 11.†

Obverse.—Scythian figure, standing to the front, casting incense into the recognised small Mithraic altar. To the right a trident with pennons ; to the left a standard with bosses and streamers.

Legend, around the device, portions of the full titles of PAO NANO PAO KOPANO.

Below the left arm व/सु *Vasu,* in the exact form of character to be seen in his Mathurá inscriptions.‡ To the left, on the side of the altar, the letter स.

Reverse.—The Indian Goddess Párvatí seated on an open chair or Greek throne, extending in right hand the classic regal fillet ; Mithraic monogram to the left.

Legend, APΔOXPO,§ " half Ṣiva," *i.e.* Párvatí.

---

dated according to the Seleucidan era, and according also to the Parthian era, the 144th year of the Parthians being equal to the 208th year of the Seleucidæ, thus making the Parthian era to have commenced B.C. 248. This date is written : " Month . . . . 23rd day 144th year, which is called the 208th year, Arsaces, King of kings."

* The Roman numbers, further defined by a star (*), are used to denote such coins as do *not* find a place in the exclusively continuous *Gupta* series embodied in the Autotype Plate.

† Those who wish to see nearly exact counterparts of these types may consult the coins figured in plate XIV., *Ariana Antiqua*, figs. 19, 20. The latter seems even to have an imperfect rendering of the व *va* on the obverse, with सु *su* (formed like *pu*) on the reverse. For corresponding types see also *Journ. As. Soc. Beng.* vol. V. pl. 36, and Prinsep's *Essays*, pl. 4. General Cunningham, *Numismatic Chronicle*, vol. VI. O. S. pl. I. fig. 2.

‡ Plate XV. figs. 8, 16, 20. The *u* is not curved, but formed by a mere elongation of the down stroke of the स *s*, which constitutes the vowel, as in the case of the *u* on *Samudra Gupta's* coin No. 2 of the accompanying autotype plate VII. The omission of the *Deva* on the coins is of no more importance than the parallel rejection of the *Gupta*, where the king's name is written *downwards* in the confined space below the arm. Facsimiles of these inscriptions may also be consulted in Professor Dowson's paper on the Mathurá Inscriptions, *Journ. R. As. Soc.* vol. V. N.S. pl. IV. figs. 15, vi., &c. See also General Cunningham's remarks on Vásudeva, *ibid.* p. 195. General Cunningham proposes to amend Professor Wilson's tentative reading of *Baraono* on the two gold coins, *Ariana Antiqua*, pl. XIV. figs. 14, 18 (p. 378), into PAO NANO PAO BAZOΔHO KOPANO. The engraving of No. 14 certainly suggests an initial B in the name, and the AZ and O are sufficiently clear. We have only to angularise the succeeding O into Δ to complete the identification. These coins have a reverse of Ṣiva and the Bull.—*Arch. Rep.* vol. III. p. 42. Dr. Kern does not seem to have been aware of these identifications when he proposed, in 1873 (*Rêvue Critique*, 1874, p. 291), to associate the Mathurá Vásudeva with the Indo-Sassanian Pahlvi coin figured in Prinsep, pl. VII. fig. 6. *Journ. R. As. Soc.* vol. XII. pl. 3 ; *Ariana Antiqua*, pl. XVII. fig. 9.

§ APΔOXPO, Ard-Ugra. The latter is the name of Ṣiva. The preceding Khadphises Indo-Scythians had, for

Ghaṭot Kacha.

No. 1. Plate VII. Gold, weight 116 gr. Very rare. B. M.

[*The numbers prefixed to these coins correspond, without break or interruption, with the serial order of the numbers entered in the accompanying Autotype Plate. The extra or casual specimens are marked by Roman figures, with a further discriminating* ✻.]

Obverse.—The King standing to the front, clothed very much after the manner of his Indo-Scythian predecessors.* The right hand casts incense into the conventional diminutive Mithraic altar, while the left holds the typical standard of the rayed Sun.

Marginal legend imperfect.

Under the arm { का *ká.* / च *cha.*

Reverse.—*Párvatí* holding a lotus flower in the right hand, with a cornucopia of western design on the left arm. In the field, the Indo-Scythian monogram.†

Legend.—सर्वराजोच्छेत्त *Sarvarájochchhetta.* "The exterminator of all Rájas."

Samudra Gupta.

No. 2. Gold. B. M.

Obverse.—The king arrayed after the Indian fashion with a *dhotí* tightly bound round his loins, elaborate native head-dress, very large ear-rings, necklace, and armlets of chosen jewels, &c., in the act of shooting a tiger who faces him to the full front.

Legend, restored.—व्याघ्रपराक्रम *Vyághra parákrama.* "The tiger hero."

Reverse.—Párvatí with lotus flower and *Garuḍa* standard, standing upon a Dragon or some oriental type of marine monster.‡

Legend.—राजासमुद्रगुप्तः *Rájá Samudra Guptah.*

---

their reverse device, a figure leaning on a Bull (*Nandi*), regarding which Professor Wilson remarks: "The figure leaning on the Bull appears, by the breasts and protuberant hips, to be female; but it is not invariably so, and is sometimes, what it probably always should be, of an androgynous outline, the figure being that of Ṣiva and his spouse in their composite character of *Arrdha nárîṣwara*, Ṣiva half-feminine."—*Ariana Antiqua*, p. 351.

* A very suggestive note on this question is to be found in Huen Thsang: "Après la mort du roi *Kia-ni-se-kia* (Kanishka), la race des *Ki-li-to* (Kritíyas) s'arrogea encore la royauté, chassa les religieux et abolit la loi du *Bouddha*," ii. 178. These kings are subsequently spoken of, in the text, as "cette race ignoble," p. 179. The commentator adds at p. 454, vol. iii. "*Kritíyas* en Chinois *Maï-te* (hommes) achetés." (See also, i. 248.) Hiouen-Thsang, Paris edit. Cf. *dása*, *kríta*, and *gupta* under the sense of "protected," in connexion with note †, p. 11 *ante*; and also Elliot's *Glossary*, vol. II. p. 281.

† This monogram has a curious similitude to the old Egyptian symbol for the Bee which, as M. Oppert has shown, was the sign royal in the Hieratic, the prototype of *ṣarru*, שר of the inscription of Nebuchadnezzar at Borsippa. *Journal Asiatique*, 1857, p. 143. See also *Journ. R. As. Soc.* vol. I. N.S. pp. 224, 482.

‡ A similar aquatic monster may be seen below the feet of an ancient statue at Nongarh (6 miles S.S.E. of Jayanagar). "The statue is made of the red-spotted sandstone of the Sikri quarries near Mathurá."—Cunningham, *Arch. Report*, vol. III. p. 161.

No. 3. Gold. B. M.

Reverse.—King appareled in close-fitting native costume, with the Indian *dhotí*, armlets, bangles, &c., reserving unexhausted arrows for a retreating lion.

Legend.—म हराजाधिराज श्री

Ma há rájádhirája Srí.

Reverse.—The Goddess *Párvatí* seated on a lion, with fillet, lotus flower, and the usual Scythian monogram.

Legend.—श्री सिङ्हविक्रम *Srí Siṅha Vikrama.* "The Lion-hero."

No. 4. Gold. B. M.

Obverse.—A horse decked for the Aṣvamedha sacrifice.

Legend (restored).—नवजमधः राजधिराज पृथिवी जियत्य

Navajamadhah Rájadhirája Prithiví jiyatya.

Below the horse से *se.*

Reverse.—A rayed female figure (*Párvatí* ?) holding a *chaurí* or Yák's tail, ordinarily used as a fly-whisk in the train of royalty.

Legend.—अश्वमेध पराक्रमः *Aṣvamedha parákramah.* "The hero of the Aṣvamedha."

A recent contributor to the *Journal Asiatique*, has taken me to task for discovering any traces of Scythism in the Indian *Aṣvamedha* rite, and after other curious criticisms, intrenches himself in the direct assertion that "le cheval des sculptures est le cheval des légendes et du culte bráhmanique."*

To my apprehension the Indian Aryans have put on record, in their own Vedas, a much more mundane account of their notions of the Aṣvamedha sacrifice, which seems to have been little more to them than a religious feast, with all the sensual accessories of fat horse flesh, baked meats, aromas of cooking, with essays on the merits of skilful carving: descending at last into gross questions of skewers, and the stray remnants that adhere to the hands of the operators.†

Far different is the impression conveyed by what we can gather from the local conceptions of the *Aṣvamedha*; here the ideal seems to have been eminently Scythic, both in its inception and application; it was in effect a martial challenge which consisted in letting the *victim*, who was to crown the imperial triumph at the year's end, go free

* *Journ. Asiatique*, 1875, p. 126. Essai sur la légende du Buddha, par M. E. Senart. The passage to which the author takes exception is to be found in my article in the *Journ. As. Soc. Beng.* 1865, p. 57; it has been reproduced in my *Indian Weights*, p. 62.

† *Rig Veda*, ii. iii. *súktas*, vi. vii., Wilson's *Translation*, vol. II. p. 112, and note *a*, p. 121, also Preface, p. xii.—xv.; Colebrooke's *Essays*, Prof. Cowell's edit., vol. I. pp. 50, 55, 56; *Asiatic Researches*, vol. III. p. 429; Max Müller's *Anc. Sanskrit Literature*, pp. 37, 46, 357, 533.

to wander at will over the face of the earth, its sponsor being bound to follow its hoofs, and to conquer or conciliate the occupiers of all "fresh fields and pastures new" his equine pioneer chose to fancy.* Surely such a prototype shadows forth more of the conditions of the life of desert communities of the horseman class, than of the surroundings of Aryan cattle-drivers, entangled in the narrow passes of the Himálaya, or dubiously skirting the southern base of the outer range towards the plains of India in straggling companies. The original germ and development of the contrasted heroic aspect almost declares itself in associations belonging to Nomadic tribes, among whom a steed captured in hostile forays, had so frequently to be traced from camp to camp and surrendered or fought for at last.

Of course the ultimate decision of this and many other international questions, must depend upon how much of the Turánian element we are to recognize as having existed amid the occupying prehistoric races of India; a subject far too large to be discussed with advantage in this place.

Kumára Gupta.

No. 5. Gold. B. M.

Obverse.—King standing to the left, the right hand is extended as if casting incense into the small Mithraic altar, of which traces can still be recognised. The king is girt with the *Khaṇḍá* or Indian straight broad-sword. To the right the *Garuḍa* standard, to the left the initial letters of the name of Kumára, कु *Ku.*

Legend.—गमवजित्य सुचरत कुमर

Reverse.—*Párvatí* seated on a raised throne, below which are expanded the leaves of the lotus. In the right hand, the Grecian fillet, with the recognized Scythian monogram above the shoulder.

Legend.—श्री कुमार गुप्त
Ṣrí Kumára Gupta.

Mahendra Gupta.

No. II*. Gold, weight 125·5 grains. Marsden,† No. MLIX. B. M.

Obverse.—King on horseback, to the right, with nimbus, seemingly bare-headed, with long flowing curls.

Legend.—महेन्द्र गुप्त
Mahendra Gupta.

---

* Wheeler's *Mahábhárata*, vol. I. p. 377. Prof. Goldstücker has pointed out (in the *Westminster Review* or April 1868) that the passages here quoted belong to the more recent "Jaiminíya Aṣvamedha." See also Wheeler's *Rámáyaṇa*, pp. 10, &c.

† See also Prinsep's *Essays*, pl. XXIII. fig. 30, vol. I. p. 387. See also variants, pl. XXX. figs. 3, 4, 5, *ibid.* and *Ariana Antiqua*, pl. XVIII. figs. 16, 17. No. 16, has देवजगत after the *Gupta.*

Reverse.—*Párvatí*, seated on an Indian *Moṛhá*, feeding a peacock.

Legend.—अजित महेन्द्र *Ajita Mahendra.* "The unconquered king."

No. III*. Gold, weight 119 grains. B.M. (?)

This is another coin of some interest, which I doubtfully attribute to Mahendra Gupta. It may be described as follows :

Obverse.—Standing figure with spear and flowing pennons, trident, and small Mithraic altar. Outside the spear the letters म *Ma.* हे *he* On the inside प *p.*

Reverse.—Párvatí seated, with traces of the Greek ΑΡΔΟΧΡΟ.

Nára Gupta.

No. IV*. Gold. *Ariana Antiqua,* Pl. XVIII. fig. 22.*

Obverse.—King standing to the front, with Garuḍa standard on the right, and bow in the left hand. Device similar to the designs of Samudra and Chandra Gupta's coins (*Ariana Antiqua,* XVIII. 7, 8, 9, 4, Marsden, No. ML. and MLVII.), but materially deteriorated in the artistic execution.

Legend, below the left arm.—ना *Ná.*

र *ra.*

At the foot गु *Gu.* Marginal legend ?

Reverse.—The usual type of Párvatí seated on lotus leaves to the front (disclosing greatly debased art.)

Legend, restored from other specimens.†—बालादित्य *Báláditya.*

THE SÁH KINGS OF SURÁSHTRA.

The history of the Sáh kings of Suráshtra is so interwoven with the progress and final supremacy of the Guptas, that we must devote full space to the consideration of their independent rise and advance to power—as well in regard to the monumental palæographic records, in which the western coast is so rich, as in respect to the Numismatic remains of the dynasty which equally preserve marked local characteristics, and disclose instructive indications of a source and derivation other than Indian.

The inscriptions claim priority in the order of arrangement. These commence with a group of representative mural tablets which repeat the name of the presumed founder of the Sáh family, *Nahapána.* I have transcribed the first of these records in full, as furnishing a specimen of the ordinary style and motive of this class of dedicatory

---

* I formerly had doubts about the due attribution of these coins ; but now that I have examined several specimens, I concur in General Cunningham's assignment.—*Bhilsa Topes,* p. 145. The marginal legend is there quoted as *Para-madhi Raja.*

† There are three specimens in the British Museum.

epígraphs, reducing the subsequent quotations to the bare enumeration of royal names or other material data. For the preliminary materials I am indebted to a paper by Professor Bandarkar, which was presented to the London Oriental Congress of 1874, and which is now in course of correction for the volume embodying their Proceedings.

I.—*Inscription of Nahapána in the Násik Caves.*

(No. 17 of Mr. West's facsimiles.*)

"To the Perfect One! This cave and these small tanks were caused to be constructed on the mounts Triraṣmi in Govardhana, by the benevolent Ushavadáta, the son-in-law of King Kshaharáta Satrap Nahapáṇa,† son of Dínika, who gave three hundred thousand cows, presented gold, and constructed flights of steps on the river Bárnásáyá, gave sixteen villages to gods and Brahmans, fed a hundred thousand Brahmans every year, provided (the means of marrying) eight wives for Brahmans at Prabhásu ‡ the holy place, constructed quadrangles, houses, and halting-places at Bharukachchha, Daṣapura, Govardhana and Ṣorparaga; made gardens, tanks, and wells; charitably enabled men to cross Ibá, Parádá, Damaná, Tapí, Karabená, and Dáhunuká by placing boats on them; constructed Dharmaṣálas, and endowed places for the distribution of water, and gave capital worth a thousand for thirty-two *Náḍhigeras* for the Charanas and Parishads in Pínditakávaḍa, Govardhana, Suvarṇamukha, Ṣorparaga, Rámatirtha, and in the village of Nánagola. By the command of the Lord I went in the rainy season to Málaya to release Hirudha the Uttamabhadra. The Málayas fled away at the sound (of our war music), and were all made subjects of the Khatriyas the Uttamabhadras. Thence I went to Poksharaṇi, and there performed ablutions, and gave three thousand cows and a village."

Remarks.

"The first part of this inscription is in Sanskrit. The latter part contains a mixture of Sanskrit and Prákrit."

II.—*Translation of Inscription No.* 16 *of Mr. West's facsimiles, Lines* 1, 1.

"To the Perfect One! This apartment is the benefaction of Dakhamitrá, the daughter of King Kshaharáta Satrap Nahapána and wife of Ushavadáta, son of Dínika."

Continuation of Translation of No. 16, *Lines* 3–6.

"To the Perfect One! In the year 42, in the month of Vaiṣákha, the son of Dínika, and son-in-law of King Kshaharáta Satrap Nahapána, gave three thousand 3,000 to the priesthood from the four quarters residing in this cave, as capital for [providing] garments and kuṣana. Out of this sum on 1,000 the interest is three-quarters of a

---

* *Journ. Bom. Br. R. As. Soc.* vol. VII. p. 42.

† "I think upon the whole this way of interpreting the expression is more in consonance with known facts than making Nahapáṇa satrap of a king named Kshaharáta."

‡ "Prabhásu, as Dr. Stevenson says, is a place near Pattan Somnath. Bharukachchha is now known to be Broach. Daṣapura must be some place in Gujarát or in the Maraṭhí country bordering on Gujarát. It occurs in Inscription No. 1 of Mr. West's series. Ṣorparaga is Supara near Bassein. The Damaná and Dáhanuká must be rivers flowing into the sea at those places in the Tanna District. Tapí is well known. The others I am not able to identify. Rámatírtha is, I am told, a small place near Supara. Ushavadáta's charities do not seem to have gone further to the north than Gujarát, or further to the south than the northern district of the Puṇa zillah. The expedition to the south described in the inscription was occasional, the object being to assist a friendly race of Kshatriyas." (Conf. *Ind. Ant.* vol. III. pp. 100, 214, 322; vol. IV. p. 282; Yule's *Marco Polo*, vol. II. p. 353. —Damanâ is doubtless the Damaná Gánga, and Dáhanuká the river of Dehnu to the south of it.—J. B.)

hundred [*i.e.* 75] Kárshápaṇas. These Kárshápaṇas bearing interest are not to be repaid. Out of this [sum] two thousand, which is the capital bearing an interest of one hundred Kárshápaṇas is for garments. A capital of 8,000 Náḍigeras was given in Kapuráhára and the village of Chikhalapádra."

Remarks.

"From this and No. 18 of the same series it appears clear that Ushavadáta left three thousand Kárshápaṇas; two deposited with one body of weavers, bearing an interest of 100 Paḍikas or Kárshápaṇas, from which chívarikas or garments were to be provided, and one with another body of weavers, bearing an interest of 75 Paḍikas, out of which kuṣana was to be given. Lines 4 and 5 of this and 3 of No. 18 are thus consistent with each other.

We see from the above that the cave was dedicated to the use of mendicants in the year 42, and from No. 28 that Ushavadáta bestowed other charities in the years 41 and 40. What era these are to be referred to will be considered in the remarks."

III.—*Translation of No.* 14 *of Mr. West's series.*

1. Son-in-law of Satrap Nahapána ——— t.
2. Usual deeds of Ushavadáta the Ṣaka.*
3. In Chechika, city of Dáhanuká, Kekápura.
4. In each village, in Ujjayini,† Sikhá . . [eleven lines more].

---

* "This has been usually taken to be Ṣaka, as if there were no doubt about it, but it is not quite safe to do so in the mutilated state of the inscription.

† "This is not without doubt."

I quote Prof. Bandarkar's final summing up and the resulting conclusions, with a view of showing the difficulties which still environ the question of the Sáh dates. "In the first place we have the inscriptions of Ushavadáta, which mention a king of the name of Kshaharáta Nahapáṇa, who is also called Kshatrapa or Satrap. Kshaharáta looks very much like Khagárata, and the characters in these inscriptions occupy a middling position between those of No. 6 and No. 26. Kshaharáta Nahapáṇa therefore may well have been the founder of the dynasty that displaced the Ṣátaváhanas some time after Kṛishnarája. And coins of a race of kings calling themselves *Kings* and *Kshatrapas* or *Satraps* have been found in Gujarát and elsewhere, and amongst them one of Nahapáṇa himself. There are two inscriptions also in Gujarát, which mention some of these kings. Very likely therefore it was this dynasty that Gautamíputra displaced."

"These inferences would be rendered highly probable if what is known or believed with regard to the dates of these kings were made to harmonize with the similar information we have with regard to the dates of Kṛishnarája and Gautamíputra. The coins of the Satrap or Sáh dynasty bear dates, but it is not known to what era they are to be referred. For the dates of the Ṣátaváhana kings the only authorities are the Puráṇas. Though there is no very satisfactory agreement amongst them as to the names and number of the individuals composing the dynasty, the period of its total duration, given by all, nearly corresponds. Starting from the date of Chandragupta Maurya, which is generally believed to be 315 B.C., and deducting 294, the number (Wilson's *Vishṇu Puráṇa*, chap. XXIV. book IV.) of years for which the intervening dynasties reigned, we have 21 B.C. as the date of the foundation of the Ândhrabhṛitya dynasty; and going on further in the same way we have 2 A.D. for Kṛishnarája's accession; and 319 A.D. for that of Gautamíputra. Now if we take Nahapáṇa to be the founder of the Ṣaka era, and refer all the Sáh dates to that era, the information got from the caves and the inferences based on it are perfectly consistent with these dates. Nahapáṇa's career of conquest must have ended in A.D. 78, when the era began; and this agrees with what we have stated above that the Ṣátaváhanas were deprived of the province of Násik some time after Kṛishnarája. In the same manner, if the statement that Gautamíputra exterminated the race of Khagárata is true, the last of the Sáh dates must come up near enough to 340 A.D., that being the date of Gautamíputra's death, or, the end of his reign. This last date, if the era is Ṣaka, is, according to Mr. Fergusson (*Journ. R. As. Soc.*, vol. IV., N.S.), 376, in which case it would not agree with the other; but there is a mistake here. Mr. Justice Newton, whom he follows, assigns 235

Other inscriptions of Nahapáṇa at Kárlen and Junir :—

At Kárlen—
"Peace! By Ushabhadáta, the son of Díníka, the son-in-law of Rája Kshaháráta Kshatrapa Nahapáṇa."

At Junir—
"[Constructed by] Ayama, the minister of ——— Mahákshatrapa Svámí Nahapána."

The next palæographic reference to the Sáh kings is an elaborate but imperfectly-preserved recapitulation of the consecutive repairs of the dam or bridge which retained the waters of the Paleṣani river. This document Mr. Burgess will give in full both in text and translation hereafter. I have merely to anticipate it by a brief quotation, with a view to secure the continuity of my serial evidence: which in this instance, however, is only important as confirmatory of a foregone date, already suggested by the coins. The greatest interest, to us Europeans, in this long detail of the fate and fortunes of the embankment, consists in the reference to its previous restoration by the agents of Chandra Gupta *Máurya*, our classical Sandrokoptos, whose name appears on this single occasion in the whole range of Indian epigraphy. This public

---

A.D. (*Journ. Bom. Br. R. As. Soc.*, vol. IX. p. 18) to Svámi Rudra Sáh, the 25th in his list, on the supposition that the era is Vikrama's, whence it appears that he reads the figure on the coin of that monarch as 291. But if we turn to the copies of the figures given by him at page 28, vol. VII. *Journ. Bom. Br. R. As. Soc.*, we shall find that there must be some mistake as to the right-hand stroke on the mark for a hundred in the last of the three dates given under Svámi Rudra Sáh. For the first of these is 224, the middle figure being the mark for 20, since the circle has one diameter (see the numerals in the Násik Cave Inscriptions, and my paper, p. 67, vol. X., *Journ. Bom. Br. R. As. Soc.*); the second 192, the mark for a hundred having no side stroke. It is impossible then that the king, whose date is 192, should be reigning in 291. It is extremely probable that this king, No. 18 in Mr. Newton's first list (*Journ. Bom. Br. R. As. Soc.* vol. VII.), or No. 25 in his second (vol. IX.), whose date appears thus to have been misread, is the same person as No. 12 in the former or No. 19 in the latter. For the name of the individual and that of the father is the same in both cases. There is only the prefix *svámi*, "lord," in the former, which makes no difference, and the date 192 in the one case and 197 in the other. The final date of the Sáhs, therefore, is that of No. 17 (p. 28, vol. VII. *Bom. Br. R. As. Soc.*), which is 250, for the figure resembling the letter स *sa* stands really for 50, as I have shown in my paper (p. 72, vol. X. *Bom. Br. R. As. Soc.*) on the Valabhí dates. This date in the era of the Ṣaka kings is 328. About that time then, *i.e.* about nine years after his accession, the Sáhs must have been conquered by Gautamíputra. If, on the contrary, we should take the era to be Vikrama's, Nahapáṇa's date would be about 60 B.C., *i.e.* he reigned 62 years before Kṛishnarája; which, it will be seen, does not agree with the evidence of the caves, the Ṣátaváhana dynasty having been in possession of Násik in A.D. 2. In the same manner, the final date, which, according to Mr. Newton and Mr. Fergusson, is 235 A.D. on the hypothesis that the era is Vikrama's but which really should be 196 A.D. in conformity with my reading of the dates, is so remote from Gautamíputra's, 319 A.D., that he can in no sense be said to have exterminated the "race of Khagáráta." The Vikrama era will, therefore, not do. The objection brought by Mr. Fergusson against the Ṣaka is that if the dates were referred to it, the Sáhs would overlap the Guptas by a considerable period. But this period has now been reduced to about ten years, the Guptas being supposed to have come into power in 319 A.D. And a difference of ten years in the uncertain condition of our chronology is almost nothing. Besides, there is nothing to show that the Guptas obtained possession of the countries over which the Sáhs ruled in 319, or immediately after. Thus the date 319–340 A.D. for Gautamíputra, and the Ṣaka era for the Sáh dates, alone appear to be consistent with what we find in the cave inscriptions about that monarch and the Ṣátaváhana dynasty. The dates in Ushavadáta's inscriptions, therefore, viz., 42, 41, and 40, would be 120, 119, and 118 A.D. respectively."

recognition of his dominion amid the memorial records of the western coast is a new testimony to his influence in those quarters, of which we had already external evidence in his traditional treaties with Seleucus.* So also is there an importance in the distinct mention of his grandson Aṣoka, whose *proper name* is elsewhere subdued under the *title* of *Devanampiya Piyadasi* throughout the entire series of religious manifestoes he set up in so many chance places over the broad continent of India: one transcript of which appears on the eastern face of this very rock, which, as has been seen, Nature had constituted as the ready-prepared proclamation stone of successive generations.

The Sáh or Rudra Dáma Inscription, Junágaṛ.

"To the Perfect one! This Sudarṣana lake, being from Garanagar (Girinagara) . . to the foot . . constructed in its length, breadth, and height of unbroken masonry," &c.

"This work gave way in the 72nd year . . of *Rája Mahákshatrapa* Rudra Dáma, whose name is oft repeated by the great, the grandson of *Mahákshatrapa* Chastana of well accepted (propitious) name. Afterwards (?) by the Maurya Rájá Chandragupta . . his (governor?) Ṣyena Pushpagupta of Suráshṭra (?) (*rástiriya* only visible) caused to be made . . and by the celebrated Yavana Rájá of Aṣoka Maurya named Tushaspa having been repaired."

[The text then goes on to proclaim the glories of the king, the enemies he overcame, &c., and continues] "who himself acquired the title of Mahákshatrapa, who won, &c., . . . by this Mahákshatrapa Rudra Dáma," and concludes with his own account of his special work in the ultimate repair of the dam.†

The last inscription in this list, which I have to notice, is the brief record on the Jasdan pillar, which proves to be purely genealogical—and would be otherwise immaterial were it not for its mention of the ancestral "Chashtana," whose name figures in such prominence in the initial order of the coin series.

Inscription at Jasdan in the North of Káṭhiáwáṛ pránt.

"In the year 127 Bhádrapada (*month*) dark-half, 7th (*day*) of the moon, this Satra (*tank*) of Rájá Mahákshatrapa Bhadramukha Swámí Rudra Sena, the great-grandson of the son of Rájá Mahákshatrapa Swámí Chashṭana; the grandson of the son of Rájá Ksh(*atrapa*) Swámí Jayadáman, the grandson of Rájá Mahákshatrapa . . . . . . Rudra Dámá, (*son of*) Rájá Mahákshatrapa Bhadra-Mukha Swámí Rudra. Of the son of Supra Náthaka of Mánasagotra, the grandson of Khara, with brothers . . . . . ."‡

---

* Justin, book XV. cap. 4; Diodorus, book XIX. cap. 24, book XX. cap. 12; Strabo, book II. c. 1, § 9, and book XV. cap. 1, §§ 10, 36, 53, cap. 2, § 9; Pliny, vi. 17; Arrian, Ind., cap. v. Plutarch in Demetrius.

† Dr. Bhau Dáji, *Journ. Bom. Br. R. As. Soc.* vol. VII. p. 120.

‡ *Ibid.* vol. VIII. p. 235.

COINS OF THE SÁH KINGS.

Thus much for the inscription data, we must now fill in the canvas with the more expanded revelations of the coins. As I have not been able in the brief period which has chanced to intervene between the commencement of the present chapter and its call for the press, to re-examine the conflicting bearings of the evidence affecting the domination of the Sáhs, I content myself with reproducing the latest inferences of Mr. Newton, who from the first has exclusively devoted himself to the study of the Numismatic remains of this group of kings, and achieved a veritable specialité in this department. Though in making these quotations I must guard myself by saying that I by no means invariably concur in the interpretations or deductions of the author.

Mr. Newton, in one of his latest papers, has had to review, and in some cases to revise my own early contributions to this subject,* I am the more anxious therefore that he should be heard in his own words. He says in all frankness, "The arrangement (of the dates) having been thus discussed and fixed, there remains the determination of the era to which the dates on the Sáh coinage are to be referred. Professor Wilson, in his *Ariana Antiqua*, was able only to state the priority of the Sáhs to the Guptas, but he could not restrict the rule of the latter within smaller limits than 'from the second or third to the seventh century of our era.' Mr. Thomas in his article published in 1848, in the XII. vol. of the *Journ. R. As. Soc.* (to which I have been, in many respects, much indebted), being compelled by the supposition, then entertained, that the first numerals on all the Sáh coins represented 300, was led to reject eras, which would otherwise doubtless have appeared preferable, and to select that of Ṣrí Harsha, dating 457 B.C., made known to us by Albírúní, as the one which seemed best to meet the apparent requirements of the case. . . . . Mr. Thomas thus placed the Sáh dynasty between about 170 and 50 B.C., and Mr. Prinsep placed the last member of the series in 153 B.C The initial numerals being now read as 100 and 200, the era of Vikramáditya at once suggests itself as the one to be preferred."†

Proceeding upon these principles Mr. Newton subsequently framed the subjoined list of the Sáh kings, in which he was able to insert the names of six newly identified monarchs.

1. Nahapána, B.C. 60 or 70.
2. The unknown King whose coin is given as figure 10 of the plate (p. 4, *Journ. Bom. Br. R. As. Soc.* vol. IX.)
3. (Syamo ?) tika.
4. Chashṭana, son of Syamotika, B.C. 10 or 20.
5. Jaya Dámá, son of Chastana.
6. Jiva Dámá, son of (Dámá ?) Ṣri, A.D. 38.
7. Rudra Dámá, son of Jaya Dámá.
8. Rudra Sinha, son of Rudra Dámá, A.D. 45–47.
9. Rudra Sáh, son of Rudra Sinha.

---

* *Journ. R. As. Soc.* vol. XII., 1848, p. 32.

† *Journ. Bom. Br. R. As. Soc.* 1862, p. 30.

10. Ṣri Sáh, son of Rudra Sáh.
11. Sangha Dámá, son of Rudra Sáh.
12. Dámá Sáh, son of Rudra Sinha.
13. Yaṣa Dámá, son of Dámá Sáh.
14. Damajata Ṣri, son of Rudra Sáh, A.D. 97.
15. Vira Dámá, son of Dámá Sáh.
16. Iṣvara Datta.
17. Vijaya Sáh, son of Dámá Sáh, A.D. 115.
18. Dámajata Ṣrí, son of Dámá Sáh.
19. Rudra Sáh, son of Rudra Dámá, A.D. 131, 141.
20. Viṣva Sinha, son of Rudra Sáh, A.D. 143.
21. Atrí Dámá, son of Rudra Sáh, A.D. 153, 157.
22. Viṣva Sáh, son of Atrí Dámá, A.D. 160, 168.
23. Rudra Sinha, son of Svámí Jiva Dámá, A.D. 173 or 213.
24. Yaṣá Dámá, son of Rudra Sáh.
25. Svámí Rudra Sáh, son of Svámí Rudra Dámá, A.D. 223, 235.
26. Svámí Rudra Sáh, son of Svámí Satya Sáh.*

I shall reserve any comments or observations upon the still vexed subject of the era to which these coin-dates belong, till I come to compare the entire range of recorded time-marks supplied by the more recent archæological discoveries; but I may remark, parenthetically, that the A.D. 235 of the twenty-fifth king in the above list, comes into conflict with the age I am disposed to assign to the Guptas under the Ṣaka test.

As to the correction in regard to the increase of the values of the sign for hundreds by the addition of side strokes, I long ago arrived at a similar conclusion, having, indeed, myself first suggested the probability of such a method of augmentation which the materials available in 1848 did not suffice definitively to establish.†

* "The inscriptions do not tell us that Nahapána had a son, and I have not inserted the name of his son-in-law as he is not shown to have succeeded to the sovereignty. For the same reason I have omitted the name of Chashtana's father. It is given on the coin, but we do not know that he reigned. Though no coin intermediate between Nahapána and Chastana has yet been found, I am sure that several years intervened between them. The difference of type and execution observable between their coins is certainly greater than that which exists between that of the former and the coins of the Indo-Bactrians. I have, therefore, adopted a longer interval, and hope that coins of at least two or three kings between Nahapána and Chastana may yet be found. It does not appear that Nahapána's or Chastana's coin bore a date, and it is almost certain that none was marked on the copper coin of Jaya Dámá. If the interval which I have placed between Nahapána and Chastana and the reigns which I have assigned to Chastana and Jaya Dámá be considered too long, I should be led to shorten these rather by assigning to them and all the subsequent sovereigns of the Sáh series earlier dates than by bringing down Nahapána to a time further removed from the Indo-Bactrians.

"I see no reason to modify in any respect the results arrived at in my paper of 1862 as to the succession of the Guptas to the Sáhs, the Valabhi kings to the Guptas, and the Indo-Sassanians to the Valabhí line.

"The limits of the Gujarát sovereignty in Nahapána's time must now be extended beyond the territories which I was enabled in the paper above referred to to assign to the dominion of the Sáhs. The extent, however, of the districts held in subjection probably varied from reign to reign."

† *Journ. R. As. Soc.* vol. XII. p. 37. See also *Journ. As. Soc. Beng.* 1855, p. 569, and the Paris *Journal Asiatique*, 1863, p. 383.

THE SAH KINGS OF SURASHTRA.

NAHAPANA.

No. 6. Silver; weight 31 gr. *Unique*, trilingual. MR. NEWTON.*

OBVERSE.—King's head to the right, with rough hair bound with a fillet. Very coarsely executed.

Legend, imperfect Greek.—*τυ*PANN

REVERSE.—A crude spear, with an axe on the side,† and an Indian definition of a thunderbolt?

Legend, in BACTRIAN-Páli characters, reading from the right, commencing below the point of the spear, נהפנש NAHAPANASA, following which, reading from the inside, but in the reverse direction, in INDIAN-Páli letters, नहपनस *Nahapanasa.*

The engraver or designer of this die was evidently more conversant with the outlines of the Bactrian alphabet than he was with the forms of the character of the concurrent system of writing of Indian origin.‡ The repetition of the letters of the name of the King in the latter alphabet, retain so much of the appearance of Bactrian writing, that at first, I imagined the line of the legend followed uniformly on to the left of the Semitic version of the leading name; whereas there is an obvious break in the continuity of the legend, and a complete reversal of the run of the alphabetical signs, a system

* Mr. Newton's description of this coin is to be found in Mr. Burgess's text, p. 16.

† The custom of placing the axe half way down the staff was common with the Indo-Scythians, see Kadphises series, *Ariana Antiqua*, pl. X. figs. 12–21., and pl. XXI. fig. 19. Prinsep's *Essays*, pl. VIII., &c.

‡ Mr. Burnell, in his elaborate review of "South-Indian Palæography" (Mangalore, 1874), has naturally had to refer to the earlier types of the alphabets of Northern India, regarding which our views to some extent differ. The author has quoted certain passages from a foot-note of mine, published in the Vth volume of the Journal of the Royal Asiatic Society, N.S., p. 420. This is not the place to enlarge upon subordinate transitions of alphabets extending over some centuries, but I wish to explain, in reply to Mr. Burnell's queries, that my inference regarding the Turánian or quasi-Dravidian origin of the *láṭ* character of Aṣoka's inscriptions does not imply a copying or imitation of any given Tamil *alphabet*, and far less so of the modern form now current; my object in giving the series of the *romanized* letters of that alphabet was merely to show what letters were required, and what were not required, to express *one* group of Dravidian languages. I estimate Mr. Burnell's services to the cause of Indian archæology so highly that I trust he will do me the honour to read what I have elsewhere written upon these subjects, when he may discover how little we really disagree on most points, though I certainly should object to the evidence of Aṣoka's monuments, as found in two separate sets of characters of 250 B.C., being tried by the test of the *Vaṭṭeḻuttu*, in which the author detects "most points of resemblance to the Sassanian of the Inscriptions" [of A.D. 226–384] (p. 41).

As I write a curious item of testimony as to the guiding and abiding influence of the old Aṣoka letters comes to us from Ceylon in the letter on Dr. Goldschmidt's report on the "North Central Inscriptions" of that island, published in the *Academy* of 20th November 1875, in which he says, "by finding the links between the old Indian [*i.e.* Aṣoka Láṭ] alphabet and the modern Siṁhalese, I was enabled, after a short time, to decipher inscriptions of all ages."

of definition equally maintained in the coin of Chashtana (No. 7), where, on the other hand, the Bactrian characters were subordinated and evidently left to the mercies of Indian die-cutters trained in the conventional schools of their own land.

It is interesting to observe the conjoint employment of the two *local* alphabets, in concurrence with the fading lines of the Greek, and the retention on both these coins, in a subsiding degree, of the Bactrian system of writing which marks its erratic spread into Suráshtra, following probably the line of the Indus downwards from Bháwalpur,* hitherto the lowest point to which its presence could be traced with any degree of certainty.

Chashtana.

No. 7. Silver; weight 23 gr. *Unique.*—Legends, in *three* different characters.
Mr. Newton.

Obverse.—King's head to the left, with flat cap and well executed profile.

Legend, imperfect Greek.—τυρANN.

Reverse.—A *chaitya*, composed of superimposed arches, with a demilune capital. Wavy line below; above a well-defined sun to the right and moon to the left.

Legend,† in Indian-Páli.—रञ्ञ महक्षत्रपस . . . जतिक पुत्रस चष्टनस גְשְׁתְנְשׁ
Rajno mahakshatrapasa . . . jatika putrasa Chashṭanasa—Chastaṇasa.‡

Any attempt at the decipherment of the Greek legends on these two coins has hitherto, perhaps wisely, been avoided. But I have so often found myself indebted to numismatic hints, extending even to the right appreciation of single letters, that I feel bound to put on record even my own short-comings in this instance. The materials it will be seen, are not very promising, but I may mention that the accompanying Autotype Plate only represents copies of copies§; short of the coins themselves, I have before me first reproductions in electrotype, and photographs taken direct from the originals in the possession of Mr. Newton, so that my decipherments may possibly appear in advance of my ostensible illustrative proofs.

---

* See inscription of Kanishka, *ante*.

† Mr. Newton's reading of this legend, in July 1868, was "Rajno Mahakshatrápasa (Syamo?)tika putrasa Chastanasa (ḍala?) ramna." He did not detect the repetition of the name in the Bactrian character. General Cunningham subsequently improved Mr. Newton's decipherments, remarking, "I notice that the native legends of the coins of Nahapana and Chashtana have only been partially read . . . It seems to me from the engravings that the names of both rulers are repeated in Aryan-Páli. Thus the legend on Nahapana's coin appears to me to be *Chatrapa Nahapanasa*, perhaps *Chatrapa putrasa;* and on Chashtana's coin I read *Chashtanasa* in Aryan-Páli. The Indian and Aryan names are brought together."—*Journ. Bom. Br. R. As. Soc.*, vol. IX. p. cix.

‡ Repeated in Bactrian-Páli. The Hebrew type will only imperfectly render the adapted Aryan letters of their common Semitic prototype. I have *pointed* the consonants after the system of Michaeli.

§ *i.e.* the plaster casts here photographed have themselves been taken from electrotype reproductions of the original coins, which I was favoured with by Mr. Newton some years ago.

The only letters which strike the eye, at the first glance, are ANN above the king's head in No. 7, and in the same position in No. 6, we can trace in coarser outlines the forms of PANN and a possible Υ before the P. Reverting again to No. 7, as exhibiting the best cut characters though they depart more obviously from normal Greek forms, we have a suggestive O after the second N, but the concluding letter or letters are only vaguely preserved in either specimen. The next point to determine is whether the legend should be assumed to run round the central device in one uniform line, as is the exceptional case in some of the Bactrian coins,* or whether we should look for a break in the continuity, consequent on the insertion of the King's name at the foot of the bust, which is the more constant rule in the Greco-Bactrian currencies.

The balance of evidence—apart from the reverse coincident testimony—would preferentially lead to the latter conclusion. The opening N in the name of *Nahapana* is sufficiently pronounced in its top lines under such conditions; but what then is to be said of the prefix to the possible τυραννου representing in space 6 or 7 letters, and what is to be understood to follow that title to the right in the circular legend? These are, perhaps, questions that had better be left for future solution under the auspices of better numismatic specimens, but thus much may be indicated from the struggling letters which seem to complete the list of titles that they may possibly represent in a degraded form ΣΡΑΤΙΧΙΟΥ for στρᾰτηγός, or, assuming a still greater failing in the local definition of the Greek alphabet, a more directly imperfect rendering of the title of ΒΑΣΙΛΕΩΣ which commends itself under a closer examination of the prominent letter X which may easily be reduced to an MS. Greek λ.

An important branch of the general inquiry here presents itself as to the course and survival of the Greek alphabet in India, which followed the conquering progress of the Bactrian Hellenes, as the affiliated alphabet of Semitic origin attended the more complete domestication of the Ayran races. The accessory incidents differed, however, in this respect, that the Greek language was reserved more exclusively for the ruling classes during their ephemeral sway, though its literal system was preserved in a degraded form, obviously beyond the duration of the currency of the Semito-Aryan character. Its geographical extension may be defined as nearly parallel to that of the Aryan writing towards the Gangetic provinces, while it penetrated in a comparatively independent identity to the Western coast. It is singular that there is no trace of any solitary inscription in the Greek language in India, which might, however, easily be accounted for; but, in its numismatic form it remained the leading vehicle of official record, with a subsidiary vernacular translation, during more than two centuries under Greek and Scythian auspices. It was similarly employed in conjunction with Aryan legends by the Kadphises Indo-Scythians (*Ariana Antiqua*, pl. X. figs. 5, *et seq.*), while the Kanerki Horde used it solely and exclusively in the definition of their barbarous titles (*Ariana Antiqua*, pls. XII., XIII., and XIV.) The gold coins of the latter merge into those of our Guptas, but the degraded Greek, as we have seen, gives place to a cultivated type of Indian-Páli letters.

Alexander's (Greek) colonies settled in India must have been both numerous and important, if as Arrian (Justin, xiii. iv.) and Orosius (iii. c.) declare they were erected

* Antimachus, *Ariana Antiqua*, plate II. fig. 15; Menander, do., plate IV. fig. 1; Apollodotus, do., plate IV. fig. 15; Prinsep's *Essays*, plates XIV. fig. 1; XV. fig 3.

into an independent charge under Python the son of Agenor, on the distribution of the provinces after the death of the conqueror. Later on, we have evidence of the retention of this political organization in the Indo-Greek contingent, under Eudamus, which joined Seleucus with horse, foot, and 120 elephants (Diod. Sic. xix. 1).

The mention of Antiochus and the four Greek kings by name,* in the edicts of Aṣoka, would also imply an intercourse more or less free, between the East and the classic West, coupled with the incidental use of the Greek language in states within or adjoining Indian boundaries. And the settlement of the Bactrian kings must largely have encouraged the domiciliation of Greek adventurers and with it the renewed continuity of the use of their language.

Our coins have long since testified to the occupation of the districts around Mathurá by the Bactro-Greeks, and Sanskrit texts have recently established the extension of their conquests to Sáketa (Oude) and Palibothra (Patna).†

Incidentally we learn from the Indian Embassy to Augustus (22–20 B.C.) that the credentials of the emissaries were written on parchment (διφθερα) in the name of Porus and in Greek (*Journ. R. As. Soc.* XVII. p. 309), the very mention of the employment of skins indicating a custom opposed to Indian predilections.

---

* General Cunningham has lately published an admirable fac-simile of a portion of the Indian-Páli Inscription at Khalsi (*Archæological Report*, vol. I. p. 247), and an improved eye-copy of the XIII. tablet of the Semitic Aṣoka edict at Kapur-di-giri (vol. V. p. 20). These revised texts are valuable in the geographical sense as suggesting new identifications; and the clear mention of *Andra* is of considerable importance in fixing the epoch of a race of kings about whose period there has been much discussion. I have, therefore, tentatively transliterated the joint texts and added the parallel fragmentary version from Girnár.

TRANSLITERATIONS OF THE AṢOKA INSCRIPTIONS OF KAPUR-DI-GIRI, KHALSI, AND GIRNÁR.

1. *Kapur-di-Giri.* Antiyoka namá Yona raja paran cha tenan Antiyokena chatura IIII rajano Traramaye
2. *Khalsi.* Antiyoga náma Yona . . lan chá tena Antiyo . ná chatali + lajane Tulamaye
3. *Girnár.* . . . . . Yona raja paran cha tena . . . chapṭena [*sic*] rajano Turamáyo

1. *K.* namá Antikina namá Máka namá Alikasandaro namá nicham Choḍa, Panḍa,
2. *Kh.* náma Antekina . . náma . . Máká . . náma Alikyasadale náma nicham Choḍa, Panḍiya,
3. *G.* cha Antakana . . cha . . . Magá . . cha . . . .
1. *K.* Avam Tambupanniya hevammevamhena raja Vishatidi Yonam Kamboyeshu Nibha Ka
2. *Kh.* Avam Tambapaniyá hevameváhevamevá . . . . lájá Vishmavasi Yona Kambojasu Nábha Ku
3. *G.* . . . .

1. *K.* nabhatina Bhojam Piti Nikeshu, Andrapulideshu savatam . .
2. *Kh.* nábha Pantisa Bhoja Piti Nikesa Adhapiladesa savatá . .
3. *G.* . . . . . ndhepirandesu savata . .

Under the Elephant *at Khalsi*, Gajatemre? *at the foot of the XIII. tablet at Girnár*: Sveto hasti savaloka sukháharo námam.

† "Then the viciously valiant Greeks, after reducing Sáketa (Ayodhya, *Oude*), Panchála-country and Mathurá, will reach (or take) Kusamadhvaja (Palibothra); Pushpapura (Palibothra) being reached (or taken) all provinces will be in disorder, undoubtedly." . . "The fiercely-fighting Greeks will not stay in Madhyadeṣa; there will be a cruel, dreadful war in their own kingdom." . . . "It appears that for a time after the Greeks, a rapacious Ṣaka, or Scythian king, was most powerful." Dr. Kern, from the Yugapuráṇa of the Gárgi-Sanhitá pp. 35, 38, 39; his Preface to the *Brihat Sanhitá* (Calcutta, *Bibliotheca Indica*, 1865). The Yugapuráṇa is assigned by Dr. Kern to B.C. 50. "We thus see that Patanjali lived in the reign of Pushpamitra" . . . and "we thus see that when this portion of the *Bháshya* was written, a *Yavana* king (Menander?) had laid siege to Sáketa or *Ayodhyá*, and Pushpamitra was reigning at Páṭaliputra." Professor Bhandarkar, *Indian Antiquary*, i., p. 299. See also ii. 59, 70, 96, and likewise Professor Weber, in *Indian Antiquary*, i. 173, 179 *note*, 239; ii. 58, 143; Goldstucker *Páṇini*, 230; Bábu Rajendralála, *Journ. As. Soc. Beng.*, 1874, p. 263.

Could we rely upon the statements of Apollonius of Tyana, they would carry us still further towards the proof of the extended currency and survival of the Greek language in India up to A.D. 50. We are supposed to discover Phraotes, king of Taxila, conversing fluently in that tongue, and Iarchus, chief of the Sophoi, is said to welcome his visitor "in Greek;" in like manner certain villagers are reported conventionally, and without effort, *or* pretence, to have used that form of speech. (*Journ. R. As. Soc.* vol. XVII., pp. 78, 81, 90.) This might perchance explain the unusual occurrence of so many numismatic examples of legends couched in current-hand Greek letters as opposed to the ordinary or what we term uncial capitals of monumental Greek, which gradually fell out of use about this period (*Ariana Antiqua*, Pl. XIV., figs. 12, 13), and finally merged into the unintelligible jumble of other Scythic examples discovered on Nos. 16 and 17 of the same plate.

If the decipherment of the four most prominent letters "PANN" of the Greek legends in the allied coins of Nahapana and Chashtana proves correct, it may open out several new lines of inquiry as to the status and position of Chashtana and his contemporaries; and in the enlarged numismatic associations, establish connecting links, both epochal and geographical, that we have hitherto scarcely dared to speculate upon.

A short time ago Mr. Percy Gardner, of the B.M., published a representative coin of a Ṣaka king named "Heraüs," of which the following wood-cut is a fac-simile, with his appended description, originally printed in the *Numismatic Chronicle*.

HERAÜS, ṢAKA KING.

No. IV.✳ Silver. B.M.

OBVERSE.—"Bust of a king, right, diademed and draped; border of reels and beads

REVERSE.—ΤΥΙΑΝΝΟΥΝΤΟΣ ΗΙΑΟΥ
ΣΑΚΑ
ΚΟΙΙΑΝΟΥ.
(Τυραννοῦντος Ἡράου Σάκα κοιράνου.)

A king, right, on horseback; behind, NIKE, crowning him."*

The assignment of this piece to Heraüs has been objected to by General Cunningham, who claims its attribution to the well-known king "Mauas," whose coins cover a large range both in number and variety of types.† It is quite true that the

* *Numismatic Chronicle* (1874), XIV., N. S. p. 161.

† General Cunningham reads the name as ΜΙΑΙΟΥ ΚΟΙΡΑΝΟΥ. See also *Numismatic Chronicle*, p. 109. Colonel Pearse, R.A., possesses a small *silver* coin, displaying the obverse head in identical form with the outline in the wood-cut. The reverse type discloses an ill-defined, erect figure, to the left, with two parallel legends in obscure Greek, the leading line, *with the title*, is altogether unintelligible, but its central letters range × ▭ΙΔΙΙΝ× or × ▭ΙΑΙΙΚ×. The second line gives a nearer approach to "Moas" in a possible initial M, followed by the letters 𐅃▭ΙΙΔΗΣ=μουδης, μοπρης, μουαης, &c.

imperfectly defined designation might be read as *Mauas*, though the additional second letter in the name is against such a rendering.*

But the difference in the style of the legends and the typical details of the piece seem to separate it from all other published examples of Mauas' money, and to connect it, in a marked manner, with the Parthian rather than the Partho-Bactrian section of the occupying conquerors of India.

To commence with the indications furnished by the legends, the unusual form of the kingly title ΒΑΣΙΛΕΥΟΝΤΟΣ ΒΑΣΙΛΕΩΝ which we now understand to imply direct administrative exercise of power, under the confessed authority of an imperial superior,† appears for the first and only time in the Parthian mintages on a coin of Arsaces XII. Phrahates III., B.C. 70–60, which may, as General Cunningham suggests, indicate his position as joint or sub-king under his father, in charge of a province of the empire, in contrast to the ΒΑΣΙΛΕΩΣ ΒΑΣΙΛΕΩΝ,‡ which he, subsequently, insisted on so emphatically in his correspondence with Pompey.§

The first example of the use of the term ΒΑΣΙΛΕΥΟΝΤΟΣ among the Indo-Parthian currencies occurs on a coin of Gondophares similar to No. 5, (Prinsep, vol. II. p. 215),‖ which is repeated on the money of Arsaces (Prinsep, vol. II. p. 217, and *Journ. As. Soc. Bengal*, vol. XI. p. 135). The coins of Mauas, on the other hand, appear to confine themselves to the ordinary legends of ΒΑΣΙΛΕΩΣ, ΒΑΣΙΛΕΩΣ ΒΑΣΙΛΕΩΝ, and ΒΑΣΙΛΕΩΣ ΒΑΣΙΛΕΩΝ ΜΕΓΑΛΟΥ ΜΑΥΟΥ.¶

Moreover on no occasion do they display the title of ΚΟΙΡΑΝΟΣ, still less that of the *unique* definition of the all-important ΣΑΚΑ of the coin of Heraüs.

The practical question then presents itself, as to whether this departure from ordinary routine, in the case of Gondophares and Arsaces, does not imply a recognition of the Imperial power held by the *nominal* head of the family in Persia, and co-relatively whether the employment of the nearly parallel form of ΤΥΡΑΝΝΟΥΝΤΟΣ does not in like manner, indicate merely executive administration and allegiance to a distant suzerain? The ΚΟΙΡΑΝΟΣ the dictionaries tell us, is simply a synonym of ΤΥΡΑΝΝΟΣ,** and we know that the Parthians were eccentric in their selection of Greek titles, the force of which they, perhaps, did not always comprehend, so that we must not criticise, too closely, any titles *a Ṣaka*, whose still more vague ideas of Greek filtered through such dubious channels, may have chosen to adopt.

---

* The Bactrian-Páli rendering of the name on the coins is invariably *Moasa*, which has been assumed to correspond with the Inscription definition of *Mogasa ;* see *ante*.

† *Journ. R. As. Soc.* vol. XX. p. 126 ; *Numismatic Chronicle*, (My article,) vol. II. N. S. p. 186 ; and General Cunningham's article, vol. IX. N. S. p. 29.

‡ Mr. Lindsay remarks, "the title of ΒΑΣΙΛΕΩΣ ΒΑΣΙΛΕΩΝ appears on the coins of Arsaces XII. for the first time since (its disuse after) the reign of Arsaces VI."—*Coins of the Parthians*, Cork, 1852, p. 21.

§ Plutarch in Pompey, § 38 ; Dio Cass. cap. XXXVII. § 6 ; Lindsay, p. 21 ; Rawlinson, p. 145.

‖ This example is as yet unpublished. The coin belongs to Sir H. Dryden.

¶ Prinsep's *Essays*, vol. II. p. 200 ; *Ariana Antiqua*, p. 314.

** "Τύραννος strictly Dor. for κοίρανος, from κῦρος, κύριος, a *lord, master*." The editors add, "the term rather regards the way in which the power was *gained* than how it was *exercised*, being applied to the mild Pisistratus, but not to the despotic kings of Persia."—Liddell and Scott. The ancient Persians must have been fully conversant with the use and meaning of the term, in the Ἑλλησποντίων μὲν τύραννοι of Darius, referred to by Herodotus IV. cap. 137, who elsewhere seems to admit that its interchange with βασιλεὺς was optional and unimportant.

It is in regard to the typical details, however, that the contrast between the pieces of Mauas and Heraüs is most apparent. Mauas has no coins with his own bust among the infinite variety of his mint devices; nor has Azas, who imitates so many of his emblems. But, in the Gondophares group, we meet again with busts and uncovered heads, the hair being simply bound by a fillet, in which arrangement of the head-dress Pakores, with his bushy curls, follows suit. But the crucial typical test is furnished by the small figure of victory crowning the horseman on the reverse, which is so special a characteristic of the Parthian die illustration.

We have frequent examples of Angels or types of victory extending regal fillets in the Bactrian series, but these figures constitute as a rule the main device of the reverse, and are not subordinated into a corner, as in the Parthian system. The first appearance of the fillet in direct connexion with the king's head in the Imperial series, occurs on the coins of Arsaces XIV., *Orodes*,* (B.C. 54–37), where the crown is borne by an eagle,† but on the reverses of the copper coinage, this duty is already confided to the winged figure of Victory.‡ Arsaces XV., Phrahates IV. (37 B.C.–4 A.D.), continues the eagles for a time, but progresses into single§ and finally into double figures of Victory eager to crown him,‖ as indicating his successes against Antony and the annexation of the kingdom of Media.¶

Henceforth these winged adjuncts are discontinued, so that, if we are to seek for the prototype of the Heraüs coin amid Imperial Arsacidan models, we are closely limited in point of antiquity, though the possibly deferred adoption may be less susceptible of proof.

Supposing this adoption, however, to have been contemporaneous, the dates B.C. 37 to A.D. 4 will mark the age of Heraüs, whereas Moas is speculatively assigned to a much earlier period.** But we must await the authoritative determination of many international complications in the annals of Western Asia before we can venture to draw definite inferences from the typical devices of the border-land of India.

I feel that no apology is needed for still further breaking the continuity of the leading subject of this paper by the introduction of a rare and important class of coins, which appear, in a measure, to be connected with the unique piece of Heraüs, while their Parthian peculiarities are associated with seemingly Indian forms of costume, which our friends in the Western Presidency may perchance identify, and further secure new numismatic specimens to aid a final decipherment. Though Russia has hitherto contributed the best of our examples,†† several have been traced to the lines of the Lower

---

* I see that the French numismatists quote the coins of Pacorus I. (joint king under his father Orodes I.), which follow western models. These coins exhibit the figure of Victory.

† Lindsay, *History of the Parthians*, Cork, 1852, pl. III. fig. 2, pp. 146–170; *Trésor de Numismatique*, pl. LXVIII. fig. 17.

‡ *Ibid.*, pl. V. fig. 2, p. 181.

§ *Ibid.*, pl. III. fig. 60; V. fig. 4, pp. 148, 170; *Trésor de Numismatique*, pl. LXVIII. fig. 18; pl. LXIX. fig. 5.

‖ *Ibid.*, pl. III. figs. 61–63.

¶ Lindsay, p. 37; Rawlinson, *The Sixth Monarchy*, p. 182.

** Wilson, 100 B.C.; Lassen, 120 B.C.; Cunningham, after 126 before 105 B.C.; Prinsep's *Essays*, vol. II. p. 173.

†† "Il y a quelques semaines qu'en Russie (au gouvernement de Perm) a été découvert un petit vase en bronze renfermant quatre monnaies en argent, dont j'ai l'honneur de vous envoyer les empreintes ci-jointes.

"A juger d'après le type de ces monnaies je serais tenté de les attribuer à quelque roi indo-scythe, mais cette supposition me semble être revoquée en doute par une autre trouvaille (faite en 1851 dans la même contrée) qui outre une monnaie du même genre contenait quelques monnaies sassanides (du VIe siècle) et des monnaies

Indus, localities which, as far as may be gathered, cannot be far removed, from the site of issue of the coins themselves.

These coins, whatever grade in Eastern history may be finally assigned to them, are of considerable typical importance in opening out an entirely fresh field of numismatic research. I must admit, however, that hitherto my success in their decipherment has not been commensurate with the bold outlines and apparent clearness of their legends. Nevertheless, I have not hesitated to put on record what little I have been able to unravel, and to follow out more largely the associations involved in the die-devices, with the aim of drawing attention to this promising subject of investigation, and in advocating a renewed search for similar specimens in public and private cabinets :* as it is well known that a single letter, on many a defaced piece, will often give the clue to a legend, comparatively complete in itself, but still wanting in the touch of legible vitality. While in the preliminary stage, I must frankly premise, that, though, in this case, almost every typical coincidence points to a near association with the Parthians in Bactria, or, preferentially, with their spread in more directly southern and western localities, the leading geographical evidence tending to a similar conclusion; yet the authoritative reduction of the ornamental scroll over the horse's loins (in No. V.) into the Kufic word نفر, would fatally reduce the epoch in point of time. The unknown letters on the margin, at the foot of coins Nos. VI., VII., VIII., have, moreover, a suspiciously current or cursive appearance, and, certainly, do not accord with the stiff and formal outlines of the freely legible *Malka*, in the opening letters of the variety of Syriac here employed. We have too many striking instances, in the series of Indian and quasi-Indian coinages, of the indigenous faculty of imitation, and aptitude in the reproduction of fixed and accepted designs, at times persevered in, mechanically, till all trace of the original fades before the eye and vanishes into thin air; so that typical resemblances and even close and seemingly immediate copies can hardly be held to prove what they would establish under other and less exceptional circumstances. Hence we may yet have to surrender the choicest of our specimens, in this limited list, to stand as a subdued monument of Bahrám Gor's visit to India, or as a still more modern sign and

---

byzantines d'Héraclius et de son fils Constantin. Puis les lettres qu'on voit sur ces monnaies diffèrent de celles qui se trouvent sur les monnaies indo-scythes."

* Since these illustrative wood-cuts first reached me, a coin similar in general characteristics to Nos. V., VI., VII., has been found in the collection of General Abbott, acquired in the Hazára districts of the Panjáb, which has recently been added to the Numismatic Treasures of the India Office. The piece in question, though it contributes nothing to our knowledge in the matter of types or legends, gives very significant hints in the direction of identities of metal which, in the greasy alloy, opens out mineral and geological connexions with Arachotian and other Nickel-using nationalities. See Apollonius of Tyana, quoted in *Journ. R. As. Soc.*, vol. XVII. pp. 72, 77 ; Strabo, bk. XV. cap. ii. § 10, bk. XV. cap. iii. § 14, and bk. XV. cap. i. § 69; Pliny, *Nat. Hist.*, bk. XXXIV. cap. ii. (§ 2, Aurichalcum, "fine copper," Oricalcum, Caiducium?), and bk. XXXVII. cap. xlii. ; Marco Polo, cap. XIV., XX.; and in these days Kenrick's *Phœnicia*, p. 206; General A. Cunningham, *Numismatic Chronicle*, N. S. vol. VIII. p. 279, etc.; with Dr. W. Flight, *ibid.*, p. 305 ; and My *Indian Weights*, p. 43.

I have lately been favoured with two new examples of this class of coin—the one from the Royal cabinet of Copenhagen, and a new piece from Russia. They must both be placed, typically, before No. VI., as the horseman is more on the move, and the general execution of the dies approaches nearer to the style of No. V. Both coins show very elaborate horse-trappings, with the quiver full of arrows behind the right thigh of the rider. The legends in front of the profile, on the obverse, seem to follow Pehlví tracings, but they are no more definitively legible than the scroll on No. V.; and the reverse legends fail to add anything to our previous knowledge.

symbol of Muhammad bin Kásim's first Arabian settlement on the banks of the Lower Indus.

No. V.* Silver. MUSÉE ASIATIQUE, ST. PETERSBOURG.

There is little or no trace of pure Parthianism in these devices, except in the peculiar tooling of the neck ornament.* The obverse head would almost seem to represent a young Indian-born Greek, who was so far reconciled to local customs as to cultivate with shaven cheeks a small moustache, and to recognise the manifest advantage of a turband. The eccentric eagle crowning the rider on the reverse may, possibly, imply a newly erected kingdom, or a more moderate extension of ancient boundaries.

The free action of the horse recalls the attitude of the front charger of the classic *Dioscuri* of Eucratides, or the single light horseman of the Baktrian Philoxenes;† but, here, the huntsman supplants the warrior, and the seat and saddle, and even the horse itself, if truly designed, are Indian, in ideal and execution, rather than imitations of Greek designs. The dog (if such it be)‡ is, also, an innovation upon any hitherto recognised medallic device. The use of the distinctive adjunct of the eagle placing a chaplet on the king's brow, as we have seen, was derived, in the first instance, by the Parthians from Roman teachings; it appears on the coins of Phraates IV. and Tiridates II. (B.C. 37),§ but soon gives way to the more natural winged figure of victory. The legend on the obverse I am as yet unable to decipher, but I must add, that I have neither seen this particular coin, nor even obtained rubbings or impressions of it. The curious ornamental scroll over the crupper of the horse has been read by my friends in St. Petersburg, who have sent me this wood-block, as the Arabic term فضل "excellence, wisdom;" but, though such an interpretation might be put upon the letters as they appear in the wood-cut, I should not at present be disposed to concur in any such rendering, though I must confess that the word in front of the king's profile looks more like cursive and comparatively modern Sassanian Pehlvi than any other style of writing of which I have knowledge.

---

* The letters on the Parthian coins are what we should call nail-headed (not arrow-headed), *i.e.*, the characters, instead of being cut out and sunk on the die, in continuous lines, are produced by a series of holes drilled in consecutive order upon the general outline of the letter, and connected more or less clearly by minor attaching links. On the coin itself these studs stand up like the nail-heads on a well-made mediæval chair. A similar system of dotting the leading outlines of the letters was in favour among the Indo-Scythians in India. An authoritative ink-tracing could by this means be followed, mechanically, with great exactness, where a free line engraving might, under the circumstances, have simply proved difficult and delusive.

† *Journal des Savants*, 1836, pl. II. fig. 5; *Ariana Antiqua*, pl. II. fig. 17; Prinsep's *Essays*, vol. II. p. 187, pl. XV. fig. 1.

‡ It may possibly be the foal following the mare.

§ Longpérier, pl. IX. figs. 8, 9; pl. X. figs. 5, 6, 7; Lindsay, pl. III. figs. 55, 56, 57.

This coin and the two succeeding specimens present us with more distinct Parthian identities. The head-dress on the obverse would, at first sight, appear to have nothing

No. VI.* Silver. CABINET OF COMTE STROGANOFF.

in common with the ordinary upright Tiara helmet of the Imperial dynasty; but, though the local turband is retained in a somewhat reduced and modified shape, the scroll-like ornament at the top, so seemingly exceptional, can be readily traced to an association with the crest pattern first introduced by Phraates II. (B.C. 136–126) and maintained in occasional use by Sanatrœces* (B.C. 77–70), finding favour among the local kings of Edessa,† and appearing, in a less formal design, on the Eastern Parthian coins of Sanabares‡ (A.D. 2). The horseman, on the reverse, is a close copy (even to the details of the double-thonged whip and occasional hooked-*ankus*, or subdued elephant-goad,) of the charger, which continued to furnish the standard device of so many monarchs of the Parthian race in Scytho-Bactria, typified in the devices of Gondophares, Abdagazes, Arsaces, &c., whose dates are roughly assumed at from about B.C. 26 to 44 A.D.; and, singular to say, we have an example of a nearly similarly outlined horse in the Parthian Imperial series *proper*, on the money of Artabanus III. (on a coin *dated* in A.D. 13), where the unkempt hair around the front face of the monarch, typical, perhaps, of the rude fashion prevailing amid the camps and tents of the Dahæ, nearly fills one surface of the coin, while his charger on the reverse, either in bone or limb, may fairly claim kindred with the stud-bred representatives of the Baktrian stables.§

The physiognomy of the king on the obverse of Nos. VI., VII., VIII., bears no analogy to the conventional Parthian portraiture, but is clearly derived from Indian ideals of the human face. The almond eye, the slight moustache, and the smooth-shaved rounded jowl, all associate themselves with Eastern models, ranging from the Kodes coins of Sistán‖ on the one side, to the Suráshtran pieces of the Sáh kings,¶ and the types special to the Guptas.** Hence, in admitting local influence in the composition of the profile, we must infer, either an entire surrender of Parthian predilections, a facile concession to indigenous art, or a confession of fealty by the established dynasty, and their recognition, as local rulers, by a Parthian Suzerain. Among the minor indications may be noticed the germ, or possibly, according to the age eventually to be assigned to the coins themselves, the later development, of the Sassanian broad floating fillet, together with the

* Longpérier, pl. V. figs. 7, 8, 9; pl. VII. figs. 4, 5.

† Bayer, *Historia Osrhœna*. Abgar's tiara, p. 130.

‡ Longpérier, pl. XII. fig. 4; My Sassanian Inscriptions, p. 121; Prinsep's *Essays*, vol. II. p. 215, note.

§ Visconti, *Icon. Greque*, pl. L. No. 2; Longpérier, pl. XII. fig. 9.

‖ Prinsep's *Essays*, vol. I. p. 337; vol. II. p. 203, pl. XIII. figs. 11, 12; *Ariana Antiqua*, pl. IX. figs. 1–5; *Numismatic Chronicle*, vol. IV. N.S. p. 210.

¶ Prinsep's *Essays*, vol. II. p. 94; *Journ. R. As. Soc.*, 1850, vol. XII. pls. I. II. p. 72.

** *Journ. As. Soc. Beng.*, and Prinsep's *Essays*, vol. II. pl. XXXVII. Nos. 16, 17, &c., *supra*.

crescent in front of the head-dress, which, though essentially Sassanian, was not exclusively so, as the Guptas alike affected the symbol.*

One of the grounds for preferring the later date for these coins consists in the fact, that the similitudes of the wave of the curl and general arrangement of the crest are undoubtedly closer, and more marked between the comparatively subsequent Parthian issues of Pacorus II.† and Vologeses IV. (A.D. 148–190),‡ than those of the primary patterns employed by Phraates II. and Sanatrœces; and the elegant leaf-scroll, pendant from the Indian turband of Nos. VI. and VII., finds a curious and almost exact counterpart in the ornamental fall at the back of the Parthian tiara introduced by the same Vologeses IV.,§ and revived or retained in use by Vologeses VI.,‖ and Artavasdes,¶ with whom the Arsacidan dynasty became finally extinct. But, here again, we must be cautious how we pronounce in favour of any definite period for these fashions, or pretend to determine priority of usage, which may have been dependent upon so many contrasted motives—old institutions, recent conquests, or pervading provincial designs, which would necessarily repeat themselves in the outlying portions of conterminous territories.

Nos. VII. VIII.* Silver. CABINET OF COMTE STROGANOFF.

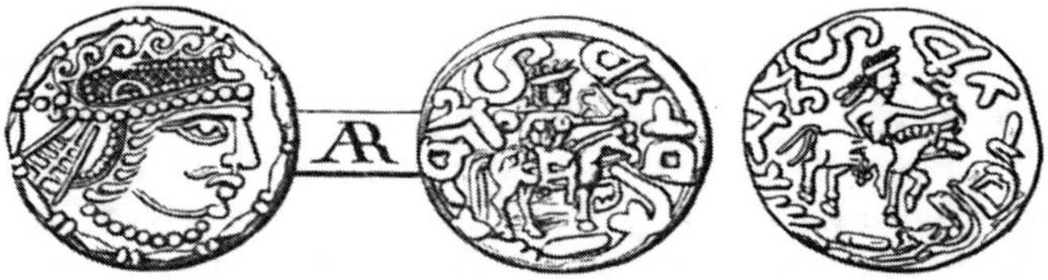

The monogram, at the back of the horseman on the reverse, offers another instance of the strange modifications ancient devices were liable to be subjected to, in the hands of artists who, probably, did not comprehend the intent and meaning of the prototype. I have felt some diffidence in identifying the odd jumble of lines on No. V. as a reproduction of the Parthian eagle; but, in truth, the original designs on the Imperial mintages, did not contribute any very exact delineation of the form of the sacred bird, and the Indian copyist may have been even less instructed in ornithology and less conversant with the flight of eagles than the Western designers; while his own local imitators may well have failed to detect a likeness he himself was incompetent to give effect to. Be this as it may, the symbol or device on Nos. VI., VII., and VIII. has clearly arrived at the monogrammatic stage, though quaint traces of the bird's head are still to be detected on Nos. VI. and VII. The monogram, in its advanced form, is assimilated to several designs in established favour with neighbouring dynasties; in its lower limbs it singularly accords with the special symbols or crypto-monograms employed by Kadphises, Kanerki and

---

* *Journ. R. As. Soc.* vol. XII. pl. II. figs. 39, 49; *Ariana Antiqua*, pl. XV. figs. 17, 18; Prinsep's *Essays*, pl. XXVII.

† Longpérier, pl. XV. fig. 6.

‡ *Ibid.*, pl. XVI. fig. 11.

§ Longpérier, pl. XVI. fig. 11; pl. XVII. fig. 7; *Trésor de Numismatique*, pl. XXI. figs. 13, 14, 17. Lindsay, pl. VI. fig. 28.

‖ Longpérier, pl. XVIII. fig. 6; Lindsay, pl. VI. fig. 31.

¶ Longpérier, pl. XVIII. fig. 11; My *Sassanian Inscriptions*, London, 1868, p. 127.

Ooerki (Kanishka and Hovishka)*; while, in its central, upper portion it approaches nearer to the Indo-Sassanian typical design, which occupies the entire coin reverse, as depicted in pl. XVII. fig. 20 of Wilson's *Ariana Antiqua,*† and otherwise, in general characteristics, it has much identity with the ordinary mystic diagrams of the Sassanian seals ‡; but both these latter may merely represent continuous imitations or developments of an abiding ideal, furnishing a fixed point of departure, which, varied in its minor details, according to the ruling conceptions or acquired tendencies of the nation, under the religious teaching dominant at the moment.

No. IX.✳ Copper. Musée Asiatique, St. Pétersbourg.

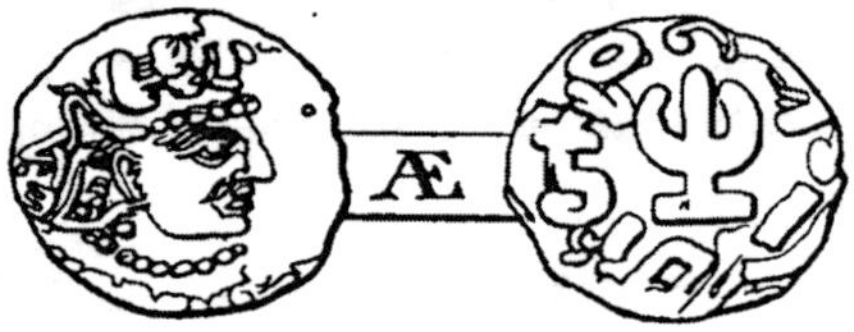

The obverse head, in this instance shows a considerable amount of degradation, even from the imperfect models, which it clearly follows. The variation in the reverse device is of moment, not only as removing the mintage from any very close connexion with its predecessors, but as shadowing forth a possible change in locality. The symbol which occupies the field belongs to one of the many forms of the Indian *Triṣula,* or trident, of *Ṣiva,*§ which crops up upon so many occasions amid the emblems of the East and the West, and which acquires an importance in the present inquiry, on account of the prominence similar devices will be seen to hold in collateral issues.‖

Having completed the incidental references to the Numismatic devices, I have to encounter the more difficult task of explaining the purport of legends.

Those illiterate savages, the Parthians, finding themselves, amid the chances of conquest, so often domesticated as alien rulers; in the absence of any alphabet of their own, very wisely accepted the casual varieties of writing current in the localities in which they held sway. Among the leading and more important systems thus adopted the following may be enumerated:—

1. *Greek,* which was taken over as part and parcel of the Court and Official language, prevailing in the dominions of the Seleucidæ, about 255 B.C.

2. *Bactrian,* or the special adaptation of a normal Semitic alphabet for the

---

* *Ariana Antiqua*, pl. X. fig. 5; pl. XI. fig. 16; pl. XIV. fig. 1; and pl. XXII. No. 155, *et seq., ante.*

† See also pl. XVII. fig. 21.

‡ *Journ. R. As. Soc.* vol. XIII. p. 425, *et seq.; Mordtmann Zeitschrift*, 1864, Nos. 63, 101, 124, 140; Lajard, *Culte de Mithra*, pl. X., numerous examples, but especially No. 13. Also plates XLV. figs. 1, 2, 4, 5, 8, 15, and plate LIV. figs. *c*, 6, 7, 8, 9–16, 19, 20, 21.

§ See coins of Kadphises (105 B.C.); *Ariana Antiqua*, pl. X. figs. 5, 12, &c.; and of Kanerki, pl. XII. fig. 4; Ooerki, pl. XIV. fig. 14.

‖ See coins No. XI.✳, &c., and note, p. 47, *infra.*

definition of an Aryan tongue, which was largely developed in India about B.C. 250, but which first appears upon Parthian coins, only in 110 B.C.

3. Various forms and modifications of Phœnician and Aramæan, employed on coins of an imitative type of the Tetradrachms of Euthydemus of Bactria (now assigned to Characene) of uncertain date; and other survivals of an old type of Syriac, such as that found on the coins of Edessa, and in allied branches of coinage of indeterminate locality.

4. The double alphabets of the ancient Pehlvi, discriminated as Chaldæan and Sassanian, which intrude among the Greek legends of the Imperial series so early as A.D. 2, and which finally supersede the Greek itself in the official records of Western Asia about the third century, A.D.

I release my Indian readers from the dry details of any attempted identification of the hybrid letters of which the coin legends V.–VIII. are composed, and simply say that I can only decipher with any pretence to certainty, the word מרכא *Marka*, for *Malka*, which commences in front of the head of the horseman, and is to be read from the *outside* of the piece. The succeeding letters seem to belong to a different alphabet, and the utmost I venture to guess at is something approaching the sounds of *Shahach* or *Shemach*,* on fig. V., which interpretation, however, is seriously shaken by the almost modern Arabic style of the letters on VI., VII., and VIII., which might be taken for لعب or لعبس

I now revert to the largely interrupted serial succession of the local Sáh kings of Surâshtra, of whose coins, however, I propose to give merely typical examples.

ÍṢWARADATTA.

No. 8. Silver. B.M.

Obverse.—The typical and "numismatically" *constant* Sáh head, in profile.

Legend, imperfect, with vague outlines of the Greek characters.—Α Ο C Ι Υ

Reverse.—The conventional *Chaitya*.

Legend.—राज्ञो महा क्षत्रपस ईश्वर दत्तस वर्षे प्रथमे.

Rájno mahá kshatrapasa Īṣwara dattasa, varsha prathame.

(*Varsha prathame*, in "the first year" of his reign?)

It still continues an unexplained mystery, why the coins of the XVI. king in Mr. Newton's serial list, p. 29, should depart from the established custom of inserting a date at the commencement of the Greek legend, and supplant it by a new form of regnal date at the conclusion of the monarch's titles and designations in the *local* character on the *reverse*.

---

* *Chach?* سیهرش صمد جاکحج. Reinaud, *l'Inde*, pp. 126, 147, 176; *Mas'audi*, vol. I. p. 342; A'in-i-Akbari, vol. II. p. 146; Elliot's *Historians*, p. 138 *et seq.*; *Journ. R. As. Soc.* vol. XII. p. 341.

VIJAYA SÁH.

No. 9. Silver. ROYAL ASIATIC SOCIETY. (Dates, according to local custom, 140 to 154.)

OBVERSE.—Sáh head as usual.

Greek legend, imperfect.—. . . IIVIIOIICVΛ

Date behind the head, expressed in ancient Indian *numeral figures*, following the initial I, 154. Confirmatory dates, 142 (Mr. Freeling's coin),* and 153 (B.M. coin).

REVERSE.—*Chaitya*, half-moon and a cluster of nine stars.

Legend.—राञ्ञो महा क्षत्रपस विजय साहस रांञ्ञो महा क्षत्रपस दामा साहस पुत्रस

Rájno mahá Kshatrapasa Vijaya Sáhasa, Rájno mahá Kshatrapasa Dámá Sáhasa putrasa.

DAMA JATA ṢRIYAH.

No. 10. Silver. ROYAL ASIATIC SOCIETY.

OBVERSE.—The usual Sáh head.

Legend, illegible. Date, in ancient ciphers, 1*7.†

REVERSE.— *Chaitya*, half-moon and cluster of four stars.

Legend visible on this coin.— . . . . श्रीय राञ्ञो मह क्षत्रपस दम

Full legend restored.—*Rájno mahá Kshatrapasa Dámá jata Ṣríyah, Rájno mahá Kshatrapasa Dámá Sáha-putrasa.*

KUMÁRA GUPTA.

Sauráshtran Series.

No. 11. Silver. MR. BURGESS.

OBVERSE.—The standard Sáh head, but much corrupted in the die execution.

REVERSE.—The goddess *Párvatí*, apparently imitated from the Eastern type of that deity, found on Kumára's gold coin, No. 5. Proving, in effect, the purport, hitherto unsuspected, of the original design, which is so strangely distorted in all other cotemporary issues. Cluster of six stars, as in the Sáh coins, but located in a new position in the lower portion of the field.

Legend.—परम भगवत महराजधिराज श्री कुमर गुप्त महेन्द्रदित्य

Parama Bhagavata Maharájadhirája Ṣrí Kumara Gupta Mahendraditya.

---

* Mr. Newton gives independent fac-similes of the dates 140 and 154, *Journ. Bom. Br. R. As. Soc.* vol. VII. p. 28.

† There is another doubtful date, of 1*4, on Dr. Stephenson's coin.

No. 12. Silver. MR. BURGESS.

OBVERSE.—The usual imitation of the typical Sáh profile.

REVERSE.—*Párvatí,* one degree less recognisable than in No. 11. Cluster of six stars, in the old position, above and to the right of the central figure.

Legend as in No. 11. Legible portion.—*Parama Bhagavata Maha . . . . hendraditya.*

No. 13. Silver. MR. BURGESS.

OBVERSE.—A totally new style of treatment of the typical Sáh head, shown in the sensual air, thick-necked profile, short curled moustache, and altered form of ear-ring.

Legend in barbarous Greek.—O NONO O, constituting a corrupt rendering of fragments of the standard Scythic legend of PAO NANO PAO. Our *Ráo* of modern days, combined with the NANO, which is referred to the masculine moon, the associate of the Babylonian NANA, NANAIA. This may possibly suggest identities, more or less remote, with the Indian *Chandra Vanṣas* ?*

REVERSE.—*Párvatí,* further degraded from the original type, but still freely identifiable. Cluster of eight stars.

Legend as in No. 11. Portion legible.—. . . . *rama Bhagavata Maharájadhirája Ṣrí Kumara Gupta . . .*

No. 14. Silver. MR. BURGESS.

OBVERSE.—The original Sáh head, but slightly modified in its details, and more closely adhering to the local prototype than the preceding examples.

Legend.—Traces of badly-formed Greek letters. The style of writing follows the unintelligible mechanical Sáh model more closely than the independently debased and free-hand Greek legend on No. 13.

REVERSE.—*Párvatí,* degraded type; with cluster of six stars.

Legend, expressed in bolder Nágarí letters than in the previous specimens. Portion of superscription visible.— . . . . *maha rájadhirája Ṣrí Kumára Gupta.*

No. 15. Silver. MR. BURGESS.

OBVERSE.—The Sáh head, debased in execution.

Legend, degraded Greek.—ONO\u.

REVERSE.—*Párvatí,* still less recognizable, but clearly following, *longo intervallo,* the established model. The cluster of stars is driven up, in the want of surface space, into the run of letters of the legend.

Legend, visible on the coin.—*Maharájadhirá . . Ṣrí Kumara Gupta.*

---

* *Journ. R. As. Soc.,* vol. XII. p. 15; *Journal Asiatique,* 1839, p. 7; *Ariana Antiqua,* pp. 358, 364; My *Ancient Indian Weights* (Marsden), p. 45. Certain gold coins were called, after the Greek name of NANO, in Sanskrit णाणक, *Ṇáṇaka's,* described as coins with the mark of Ṣiva.

No. 16. Silver. Mr. Burgess.

Obverse.—Sáh head, further debased.

Legend.—UHOU (NANO).

Reverse.—*Párvatí* further disintegrated. The Sáh stars continue to find a refuge amid the ordinary course of letters of the superscription.

Legend, expressed in coarse ill-defined characters: visible on the coin.— . . . *jadhirája Ṣrí Kumara Gupta.*

No. 17. Silver. Royal Asiatic Society. (Presented by the late Ráo of Kutch.)

Obverse.—The Sáh head, finely rendered, with an air and suggestion of Greek art.

Legend.—ONO (NANO).

Reverse.—*Párvatí,* scarcely recognizable, though the execution of the die is otherwise sharp and unhesitating.

Legend, in bold, well-cut square characters.—

परम भगवत राजधिरा · श्री कुमर गुप्त · · न्द्रदित्य

Parama Bhagavata Rájadhirá(ja) Ṣrí Kumara Gupta (Mahe)ndraditya.

This piece represents a class of money of which we have absolutely multitudes of specimens,* it has been entered in the plate, to illustrate a well understood distinction from Nos. 11–16, indicated by the absence or omission of the quasi-superlative ***Mahá*** before the "*Rájadhirája.*"

The intention of this titular discrimination, as I understand it, was to mark the relative grades of Kumára's dignity; I suppose the class of coins of which No. 17 is the representative to have constituted the currencies of the Prince while acting as Viceroy on the part of his father in the Kingdom of Guzarát. He was then a "King over Kings," but not a "*Great* King over Kings" as he became in later days on succeeding to his father's imperial throne and the position of Lord-paramount of India.†

* *Journ. R. As. Soc.,* vol. XII. p. 65.

† Objection might be taken to this conclusion on the ground that the typical degradation of the central figure on the reverse in No. 17 is greater, and evidences a more distinct departure from the prototype than the device on the coin bearing the *imperial* prefix to Kumára's name. But the character of work of the No. 17 class is better as a rule, while more local in adhering to the Sáh model, than that of the coins with the improved definition of the figure of *Párvatí,* which perhaps may have been entrusted to artists sent from the capital on the accession of the new Emperor, and who would have understood the intent and meaning of the device they had to execute better than the provincial die-cutters, who perhaps worked mechanically from their own anterior models. It will be noticed that the heads on the obverses of Nos. 11 and 13 follow different ideals, and are less finished than those on Nos. 10 and 17; and the style of the Greek character further marks a different school.

No. X.* Silver. Mr. Newton.

Obverse.— 

Reverse device similar to No. 18, Autotype Plate, and Bakra Gupta's coin, No. XI.*

One of the most suggestive coins in the entire series emanating from the Western mints is the piece here reproduced, *on wood*, from Mr. Newton's original design given in his Plate, p. 3, *Journ. Bom. Br. R. As. Soc.* vol. VII.

The coin bears the conventional imitation of the Sáh profile, with the still clearly marked system of local dating so far as the position is concerned, commencing from the base of the skull on the left, and retaining the ordinary initial prefix of the *iota* (I), whose purport is as yet unfathomed ; after this symbol, if originals and copies are not at fault, we encounter the distinct and universally accepted sign for 90 (⊕) ; following this, in the ordinary line of reading of the Greek legend, some vague outlines of a unit may be traced, which would still keep the date within the reasonable limits of Kumára's succession, *i.e.* within the full *hundred*, or up to seven indeterminate years subsequent to the inscription date of 93 of his father Chandra Gupta II.

The given 90 or any number up to 99 may be tested by three different systems of interpretation; first, under the theory of the omission of *hundreds* seen in Bactrian and other examples, but alien to the ordinary course of Suráshtran definitions; second, under the supposition of a casual default in the expression of the sign for *hundreds*, and the implication of an immediate succession by Kumára to Swámí Rudra Sáh, who concludes the series of Sáh coin dates, in the numbers 280–292, expressed in the ciphers of their own system, which would, in so far, account for the consecutive appearance of the 90 *odd* on Kumára's coin;* or, third, under the more satisfactory and conclusive inference that the number 90 had reference to the family system of dating already in use in the home dominions of the Guptas, which would curiously confirm many independent verifications of their epoch. It is, therefore, under this last head that I propose to class the formulated date in question. Thus, taking it in consecutive order with the 93 of Chandra Gupta II., Kumára must have succeeded to the throne some time before 100 of his dynastic system of reckoning and assuming this to have followed the era of Ṣaka, about A.D. 179.

No. XI.* Silver. Mr. Newton. (*Journ. Bom. Br. R. As. Soc.*) 1862, p. 3, Plate (un-numbered) Fig. 11.

Obverse.—A very straggling and chaotic outline of the Sáh profile, its defects are apparently less attributable to the ineffectual efforts of the modern native copyist than to the faulty dies of the ancient mints.

Reverse.—The device shown in the accompanying wood-cut, which has been copied implicitly by Mr. Adeney from the original in the Bombay lithograph.

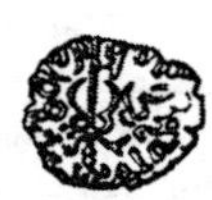

* Mr. Newton apparently advocated this view of the question (*Journ. Bom. Br. R. As. Soc.*, vol. VIII. p. 10), though he was quite clear about the absence of any cipher before the 90, and recognized the I, or, as he calls it, the "figure which appears to be a mint mark, commonly found on the Sáh coins."

Legend.—Mr. Newton, who had the original piece before him, confidently transcribed the characters as *Parama bhagavata* (*rájádhirájá*) *Ṣrí Kumára Gupta Mahendrasya.* The Kumára Gupta is clear in the wood-cut, but the device separates the piece from the ordinary issues of that King.

Bakra Gupta.*

No. XII.* Silver. Mr. Newton.

Obverse.—Sáh head but slightly varied, and still retaining the conventional ornamental collar.

Legend.—Traces of NANO.

Reverse.—Párvatí, not far removed from the type shown in No. 15 of the accompanying Autotype Plate. Cluster of seven stars.

Legend.—परम . . . . राजधिराज श्री बक्र गुप्त विक्रमादित्य

Parama . . . . rájadhirája Ṣrí Bakra Gupta Vikramáditya.

Skanda Gupta.

Suráshtran Series.

No. 18. Silver. Royal Asiatic Society.†

Obverse.—The typical Sáh head, greatly debased.

Reverse.—Párvatí reduced to fragmentary lines and dots.

Legend, in full, restored from better specimens—

परम भगवत श्री स्कन्द गुप्त क्रमदत्य

Parama Bhagavata Ṣrí Skanda Gupta kramaditya.

Visible on this coin, *Parama . . . Ṣrí Skanda Gupta kramaditya.*

No. 19. Silver; *double struck.* Royal Asiatic Society.‡

Obverse.—The Sáh head, obscured by the second impression of the die.

Legend.—Traces of NANO.

Reverse.—Figure of Ṣiva's Bull, *Nandí*, recumbent.

Legend, restored.—परम भगवत श्री स्कन्द गुप्त क्रमादित्य

Parama Bhagavata Ṣrí Skanda Gupta kramáditya.

Legible of the first die impression, *Bhagavata Ṣrí Skanda Gupta kramáditya.*
Traces of the second or superstruck die, . . *ya par* . . .

---

* Published by Mr. Newton, *Journ. Bom. Br. R. As. Soc.*, 1862, p. 11. The coin is stated to have been found in company with a collection of pieces of Kumára Gupta.

† Engraved as No. 20, pl. XV., *Ariana Antiqua.* So unintelligible was the device, that Párvatí was placed, both by the author and the engraver, upside down.

‡ See also engravings of this coin in *Journ. R. As. Soc.*, vol. XII. pl. II. fig. 45, p. 66, and *Ariana Antiqua*, pl. XV. fig. 16.

No. 20. Silver. B. M.

Coin similar to the last.

Legible, on reverse of the original piece.—*Parama Bhagavata Ṣrí Skanda Gupta.*

The recumbent Bull, *Nandi,* which figures on the reverses of these coins was adopted intact as the emblem of the succeeding dynasty of the Valabhís; hence we find it on the seals of the copper-plate grants of Ṣrí Dhara Sena* and Dhruva Sena,† which are further attested with the regal stamp of श्रीभटार्कः *Ṣrí Bhaṭárkah,* below the Bull.

No. 21. Silver. B. M.

Obverse.—The typical Sáh head, much debased.

Legend.—NAN . . . *vavo.*

Reverse.—A small Altar, which may be intended either for the Mithraic altar, figured on Nos. 1 and 5 ante, or for the conventional shrine of the sacred Túlsí tree of the Hindús.

Legend restored.—परम भगवत श्री स्कन्द गुप्त क्रमादित्य
Parama Bhagavata Ṣrí Skanda Gupta kramáditya.

Legible on this specimen, *Parama Bhagava . Skanda Gupta kramáditya.*

It is worthy of remark that this altar symbol, like the Bull of Skanda Gupta's other type of money (Nos. 19, 20), which passed on as the heritage of the Valabhís, is adopted by his Gurjjara successors as their distinctive emblem. It may be followed in its course on the copper-plate grants of Prasánta-rága, a monarch "devoted to the worship of the Sun," under the dates of 380 and 385 Ṣaka.‡ The interpretation of the parallel dates by the Ṣaka-era test seems to be almost necessitated by the discovery of a later grant of 417, to which date the words *Ṣaka Nṛipa* are subjoined.§

Ṣrí Gupta.

No. XIII*. Silver. Weight, 31 grains. Mrs. Freeling. *Unique.*||

Obverse.—The original device of the Sáh head, closely approximating to the normal outline.

Legend, in imperfect Greek.— . . ΛCIOIO . .

Reverse.—The standard *Párvatí* device, deteriorated to the extent shown in the accompanying fac-simile, with the Sáh cluster of stars and associate half moon. 

Legend.—Tentative reading.—श्री ञ्दगुप्तवक्रमद्रस्य श्रीगुप्त

* *Journ. As. Soc. Beng.*, vol. IV. pl. XL. p. 486.
† *Ibid.*, vol. VII. p. 978; Prinsep's *Essays*, vol. I. pp. 257, 262.
‡ *Journ. R. As. Soc.*, N. S., vol. I. pp. 262, &c.
§ Inscription of Dadda, whose capital seems to have been Broach. *Journ. Bom. Br. R. As. Soc.* 1871, p. 19.
|| Prinsep's *Essays*, vol. II. p. 94.

I am afraid that we must reduce the pretensions of the *Ṣrí Gupta,* whose name appears on this unique coin, from the possible position of father of the family, down to a very minor and incidental succession to the later glories of his falling race. Whatever speculations may have been encouraged by the mere discovery of the name of *Ṣrí Gupta* must now give way to the stern determination of numismatic facts. Tried by such tests the *reverse* of our specimen sinks it into comparative obscurity and carries down, with its own typical degradation, the claims of the king who issued it.

KUMÁRA GUPTA.

Peacock types.

Nos. 22, 23. Silver. My Cabinet.

OBVERSE.—A localized and greatly debased imitation of the Sáh head, especially disfigured by the Oriental rendering of the almond eye.

Legend.—In this class of coins all pretence of copying or attempting to reproduce the imitative Greek legends is fairly abandoned.

But in lieu thereof we are presented with the far more definite record of the three-figured date transposed from the ordinary position behind the Sáh head, to the less contracted space in the field, in front of the profile. In these cases the use of the indigenous ciphers, each of which expressed its own *full* number, arranged in the same perpendicular order as the initials of the royal names on the gold coins (Nos. 5, &c.), has this advantage over any system of dating in figures dependent on relative position, that in broken sequences, so inevitable in hand-struck pieces, we can pick out the *hundreds, tens,* and *units,* with absolute certainty, and combine the general result from independent specimens, without being tied down to the proof of a continuous entry on any single coin.

REVERSE.—An admirably executed figure of a Peacock with full front expanse of plumage. To the right, at the foot, a reduced cluster of three stars.

Legend.—देवं जयति विजितावनिरवनिपति कुमार गुप्तो

Dev(o) jayati vijitávanir avanipati(h) Kumára Gupto.

"His Majesty, Kumára Gupta, who has subdued the earth, rules." *

---

* When once fairly deciphered, these obscure legends will be seen to present but few difficulties. The lapidary inscriptions have already proved that the Gupta artists indulged in faulty Sanskrit orthography as well as in grammatical errors, so I need not detain my readers by any comments upon minor imperfections, while the general sense of the legend remains sufficiently clear. I must mention that, in my Devanágari transcripts, I have adhered servilely to the original legends impressed upon the coins ; the version in the Roman type has been corrected up to Sanskrit requirements, by Dr. Fitzedward Hall.

There is a superfluous य *y* (or possibly an म *m*) after the गुप्त on Skanda Gupta's coins, the use of which not apparent, but which clearly takes the place of the final *o* in Kumára's legends

I may note that Kumára Gupta's coins display both the old form of म *m* and the more specially Gupta outline of that character. (*Journ. As. Soc. Beng.* vol. IV. pl. XLIX., figs. 10 and 12.) The य *y* is also seen in its transition state from the triple-lined letter of early days to the almost modern form ; while at times it appears, on Skanda's money, as a character not easily distinguishable from the later Kumára म *m* just adverted to. This extensive modification of the य *y* in the numismatic alphabet, is the more curious, as the corresponding apidary character retains all the essentials of its ancient outline throughout the Gupta inscriptions, from the Allahábád pillar to Budha Gupta's record at Eran ; and even on to Toramána's inscription at the same place.

The range of dates on this class of Kumára coins is more complete in the units than in the tens. We have but a single example of the latter which, however, recurs frequently and constitutes unmistakeably the θ, or casual likeness of that character, which stands for 20. The units for the numbers 1, 4, 8,* 9 and entered below the θ are equally positive.

SKANDA GUPTA.

Nos. 24 and 25. My Cabinet.

OBVERSE.—Head as above. Traces of a date in front of the profile. The figure for 100 is quite plain and distinct on the original of No. 24.

REVERSE.—Peacock as above. The stars are omitted.

Legend.—विजितावनिरवनिपति जयति देव स्कन्द गुप्त य

Vijitáranir avanipati(h) jayati deva(h) Skanda Gupta-y.

BUDHA GUPTA.

No. 26. Silver.

OBVERSE.—Head as above. Date in front of the profile, 155.†

REVERSE.—Peacock as in No. 25.

Legend.—देव जयति विजितावनिरवनिपति श्री बुध गुप्तो

Dev(o) jayati vijitdvanir avanipati(h) Ṣri Budha Gupto.

TORAMÁṆA.

Nos. 27 and 28. Silver. B. M.

a. Colonel BUSH's coin ; *b.* Miss BARING's late donation to the B. M.

OBVERSE.—Gupta head, facing to the *left*, thus marking an *intentional* modification of the conventional Gupta dies.

Legend, in front of the profile, reading downwards, from the outside. 82 or rather 182, the figure for 100 is obliterated.

REVERSE.—Peacock as in the proper Gupta series, greatly debased in form and design.

Legend restored.—देव जनित विजितावनिरवनिपति श्री तोरमण

Deva janita vijitávanir avanipati Ṣri Toramaṇa.

---

* The 8 has not hitherto been quoted. It may be seen on one of the coins of Kumára, in the Stacey Collection in the Museum of the Asiatic Society of Bengal. The same collection contributes the *unique* figure of 9.

† The unit on the British Museum coin figured in my plate II. *Journ. R. As. Soc.*, vol. XII. No. 56, would seem to carry us on to 157.

Bhaṭṭaraka Kings.

Nos. 29, 30, 31. Debased silver. Mr. Burgess.

Obverse.—The Sáh head, but little modified.

Reverse.—Fragmentary traces of the design exhibited in coin XI.* and in the wood-cut of the copper coin, No. XIV.*

Legend, partially restored.—राज्ञो मह क्षत्रपरस . . . कस महस . , भट्टरकस
Rajno Maha Kshatraparasa . . . . Mahasa . . Bhaṭṭarakasa.

Nos. 32, 33. Copper.

Obverse.—Sáh head.

Reverse.—The combined form of the bow and trident, greatly obscured.

Legend. As in No. 29.

No. XIV.* Copper. Weight, 12 grains.

Obverse.—Humped Bull to the left, with a dotted circle.

Reverse.—Strung and drawn bow, with arrow projecting into a curved trident, of which it forms the central prong.

This little mite of copper proves to be worth far more than its weight in gold, for the light it throws upon the primary design of the hitherto incomprehensible device on the class of Suráshtran coins Nos. 29–33. But far beyond the mere mechanical identification of an obscure symbol is its value, in the historical sense, in the link it establishes between the Guptas, or their immediate successors, and the proximately contemporary dynasty of the nine Nágas, adverted to the quotation from the *Vishnu-Purána* (p. 11 *ante*).

The reverse devices of the Gupta Suráshtran coins have already exercised our conjectures: the Párvatí solution, in the one case, was as unexpected as the discovery of the prototype of the device of No. 29 in the simple bow and arrow combination with Ṣiva's trident, disclosed in the wood-cut.

Many and various have been the guesses as to the purport of this combination of lines on these coins. My latest impressions were in favour of a crude copy of the figure of "Minerva Promachos" of the currencies of Apollodotus and Menander, which entered so largely into the circulating media of Western India, the degraded types of which would almost have justified any shortcomings on the part of native imitators. Looking at the autotype reproductions of Nos. 30, 31, 32, 33, from the top of the page, the flowing garments and the extended shield readily suggest themselves; but now we discover, under the teaching of the independent home device, that the triṣula or special emblem of Ṣiva, whose worship is so distinctly to be traced by independent testimony, constituted the banner of the Bhaṭṭarakas, and Minerva's shield subsides into the light battle-axe of the Scythians, which is preserved in its form and relative position on the staff of so many village weapons of Northern India to this day.*

The Numismatic identifications of the currencies of the Nágas have been followed out in detail, in General Cunningham's later Archæological Reports; it will be sufficient for my present purpose, to append his remarks in a foot note.† Merely premising that the connection between the Nágas and the Western successors of the Guptas is indicated in the identity of the outline of the Bull on coins Nos. XIV.*, XV.*, and that the

---

* The presence of the triṣula or trident is an indication of the adoption of the worship of Ṣiva; and the trident, it may be remarked, is combined with an axe on one side of the staff like the tridents at Barahat and Gopeswara.—*Journ. As. Soc. Beng.*, 1836, p. 485; H. H. Wilson, *Ariana Antiqua*, p. 350, pl. X. figs. 12–21, pl. XXI. fig. 19, and Chandra Gupta coin, pl. XVIII. fig. 10.

Varieties of the *triṣúl, balá*, or trident, continued to be emblematic on the coins of the first *third* of this century in Mathurá, Jalaor, Ságar, Ṣrínagar, Kálpí, &c.

Prinsep's *Essays*, "Useful Tables," p. 67, pl. XLVI. figs. 42–46; *Journ. As. Soc. Beng.*, 1834, pl. III., "Useful Tables," p. 55.

† "If I am right in the identification of Narwar with the Padmávati of the Puráṇas, we obtain one of the most interesting and important facts in ancient Indian history in fixing the actual locality of the kingdom of the nine Nágas. The identification is strongly corroborated by the numerous coins of various Nága kings which have been found at Narwar, Gwalior, and Mathurá, all of which have been described by me in the Journal of the Asiatic Society [*loc. cit.*]. It is further supported by a passage in the 18th line of the Allahábád pillar inscription of Samudra Gupta, in which the king boasts of the extent of his dominions, and enumerates the different princes and countries which had become subject to this power. Amongst the former he mentions *Ganapati-Nága* as one of the tributary princes of Aryavartta. Now, *Ganapati* or *Ganendra* is the name of the Nága Raja, whose coins are the most common and the most widely diffused of all these Narwar kings: and as the legends of his coins are in the very same characters as those of the Gupta coins and inscriptions, it is certain that he must have been a contemporary of one of the princes of that dynasty. I think, therefore, that there is every probability in favour of the identity of the Ganapati-Nága of the Narwar coins with the Ganapati-Nága of Samudra's inscription. My discovery of an inscription of Samudra Gupta in Mathurá itself is sufficient to show that the Nágas must have lost their dominion over that city at least as early as the reign of Samudra."

"The period to which the nine Nágas must be assigned depends solely on the date of their contemporaries the Guptas, whose power became extinct in A.D. 319. If, therefore, we refer the rise of the Gupta dynasty to the Saka era, the date of Samudra Gupta will fall in the first half of the second century of the Christian era. But as in his reign the power of the Nágas had already begun to decline, I think that the establishment of the Nága dynasty may be fixed with some certainty about the beginning of the Christian era. According to this view, the rule of the nine Nágas would have extended over the whole of the first and second centuries, or from A.D. 0 to 225. In the following list I have arranged the names of these Nága Kings according to the devices of their coins, beginning with those types which seem to me to be the earliest on account of the more ancient appearance of their accompanying inscriptions. It is worthy of note, as corroborative of the date which I have assigned to the Nágas, that the whole of the devices of their coins are to be found also on the silver coins of the Guptas themselves, or on those of their acknowledged contemporaries:—"

No.	A.D.	Names on Coins.	Devices.
I.	0	Bhima Nága - - - - - -	Peacock to the left.
II.	25	Kha* Nága (? *Kharjjura*, or *Kharpara*) -	Ditto to the right.
III.	50	Va* Nága (? *Varma*, or *Vatsa*) - -	Ditto ditto.
IV.	75	Skanda Nága - - - - - -	Ditto ditto.
		Ditto - - - - - -	Bull recumbent to the right.
V.	100	Brihaspati Nága - - - -	Ditto ditto.
VI.	125	Ganapati, or Ganendra - - - -	Bull as in coin No.
		Ditto - - - - - -	A wheel.
VII.	150	Vyághra Nága - - - - -	Ditto.
VIII.	175	Vasu Nága - - - - - -	Ditto.
IX.	200	Deva Nága - - - - - -	Ditto.
		Ditto - - - - - -	Bull recumbent to right.
	225	Ditto - - - - - -	Triṣula.
		Close of the dynasty.	

association of the Nágas with the central Indian Guptas is more distinctly shown in the annexation by the latter of the typical Peacock of the first-named dynasty, who, singular to say, latterly abstained from its use, and adopted the new device of the Bull under Skanda Nága.*

Ganapati Naga.

No. XV.✳ Copper. Weights (in full currency order) average 36·4, 18·2, 9·1 grains.† Prinsep's *Essays*, pl. VIII. fig. 9, pl. XXXIV. fig 31, *Journ. As. Soc. Beng.*, 1834, pl. XXVI. fig. 9, 1865, pl. XVIII. figs. 7, 8, 9.

Obverse.—Bull, as in the coin above figured (No. XIV.✳), with a margin of dotted lines of identical design.

Reverse.—No devices. The field is filled in with the circular legend.

Legend restored.—श्रीगणपत्य
Srí Ganapatya.

Pasupati.

No. XVI.✳ *a.* Copper. Weight, 92 grains. Fig. 15, pl. XVIII., *Journ. As. Soc. Beng.* 1865, p. 115; and Prinsep's *Essays*, pl. XXVIII., fig. 23.

Obverse.—Figure of the King seated cross-legged in the Indian fashion, his right hand holding a flower, and his left resting on his hip; the whole surrounded by a circle of large dots.

Reverse.—A vase surmounted by a crescent and star, or perhaps a flower, and enclosed in a circle of large dots.

Legend, in Gupta *Nágarí* characters.—पशुपति
Paşupati.

No. XVII.✳ *b.* Copper. Weight, 92 grains. Fig 17, *ibid.*

Obverse.—A short trident or *trisul*, on a stand surrounded by a circle of small dots.

Legend in two lines.—
प शु *Pa şu*
प ति *pa ti*

Reverse.—The sun, with prominent rays surrounded by a dotted circle.

Legend as in Obverse.

"As the Nágas would appear to have been tributary to the Guptas in the time of Samudra, I think it most probable that the kingdom or district of Narwar must have remained subject to them, until near the close of their dynasty, about A.D. 275, when their sovereignty to the south of the Jumna fell to Toramáṇa."

"Of Toramáṇa's dynasty we have two inscriptions, one of himself at Eran to the south of Narwar, and the other of his son Pasupati at Gwalior to the north of Narwar. From the relative positions of these inscriptions we may fairly infer that the intermediate country must also have belonged to the Toramáṇa dynasty. The date of Toramáṇa himself is fixed by Mr. Thomas on the authority of a silver coin to the year 180" [*proved* by the second example in the plate from, No. 28] "odd of the Gupta era, which referred to the initial year of Şaka would place him in A.D. 260. If, then, we allow twenty-five years to each generation, the reign of Toramaṇa will range from 260 to 285 A.D., and that of his son, Pasupati, from 285 to 310 A.D."

* *Journ. As. Soc. Beng.*, 1865, pl. XVIII. p. 120.

† These coins are common and abundant in the extreme. Colonel Stacy's collection alone contained no less than 3479 specimens; and General Cunninghm mentions that he has acquired, at various times, many more than 3000."

Résumé.

The description of the Gupta coinage, with its provincial ramifications, in unstinted array, has now been extended, far beyond my original design, in the previous pages.

The critical observer of my text will notice an apparent absence of method, leading me to expand on the one part and contract on the other the general scope of my annotations. These anomalies have been chiefly due to the uncertain demands of a printing office in England, and the irregular reception of editorial sanction from the Archæological Surveyor of the Western Presidency, who is once again at his post, occupied with the duties of a new season's operations. Thus, as chance would have it, I have had ample opportunity of completing progressively certain minor details, but find myself limited in point of time, at the last moment; so that I have had to withdraw, perhaps, the most interesting chapter of the whole series, consisting of a comprehensive essay on the source, progress, and development of the ancient Indian numerals, as well as to defer a more complete review of Indian dates as rectified or confirmed by the numismatic evidence above submitted; so that I have had to reduce my recapitulation of the Gupta and other international dates to the abstract form embodied in the subjoined table, which however effectively combines most of the existing data available for the scrutiny and ultimate adjustment of independent commentators.

Abstract of the Recorded *Gupta Dates.*

Names of Kings.	Inscriptions.	Coins.	Tradition.	Result, A.D., derived from the Saka Era.	Remarks.
1. Gupta - -					
2. Ghaṭot Kacha -					
3. Chandra Gupta I. -					The first Mahárájádhirája.
4. Samudra Gupta -					
5. Chandra Gupta II. -	82 93		Reigned 23 years after the conquest of Suráshtra.	161 172	
6. Kumára Gupta -		90 odd 121 129		? 200 208	Coin of Kumára, No. X.*
7. Skanda Gupta -	130 138 141 146		Reigned 20 years. Senápati Bhaṭṭaraka, two years before Skanda's death.	209 217 220 225	
8. Budha Gupta -	165	155		234 244	
Toramáṇa - -		182		261	
Other local *unrecorded* Gupta Kings.					
Vallabhís - -				319	The first even nominal *Mahárája* in the irregular dynastic lists is the third *Senápati.* The VIIth ruler, in the same order, seems to have been the earliest Monarch of any real pretensions.

COINS OF THE ARABS IN SIND.

Some of the less prominent examples among Mr. Burgess's recent acquisitions may possibly prove of more direct and immediate interest to Antiquarians in Western India, than the numismatic remains of unrecorded history with which we have hitherto been concerned.

The conquest of Sind by the Arabs, in A.H. 93 (A.D. 712), constitutes a marked epoch in the annals of the land, and is associated with many instructive coincidences—in its inception, in the domestication of the conquerors on an alien soil, and their abrupt disappearance into comparative obscurity.

The daring and chivalric advance of Muhammad bin Ḳásim, was freely backed by the encouragement and support of the celebrated Hijáj bin Yúsaf, who so completely reversed the Khalif 'Umar's policy of non-extension of the Muslim boundaries to the eastward.

It is curious to note the readiness with which the conquerors settled themselves as residents and the facile refuge this extreme corner of the Muhammadan world afforded to persecuted or heretical members of the new faith, while they retained among themselves so many of their ancient tribal divisions and jealousies; and it is instructive to follow the untold tale of ethnic subsidence and final absorption into the Indian native element, when the true Arab blood came to be exhausted by foreign admixture, as in other cases wherever the standard of the Prophet carried with it, the loose teachings of polygamy, beyond the nomadic tents of the desert.

The sole preface to such obscure investigations as the present must be gleaned from the casual contributions of Arabian writers to the annals of an outlying province, with which they were seldom brought in contact.

In the subjoined table of the Arab rulers of Sind, I have taken, as my leading authority, a writer, who seems to have had extensive and exceptional knowledge of his subject. This list was originally compiled from Reinaud's text and translation of *Belázarí* for my edition of Prinsep's Essays, being further collated with Sir H. M. Elliott's excellent work on the Arabs in Sind, which has since been incorporated in his *Historians of India*, vol. I. p. 113.

A.D.	A.H.		
711–712	93	1.	Muḥammad bin Ḳásim.
		2.	Yazíd bin Abú Kabshah *as-Saksakí.*
714–715	96	3.	Ḥabíb bin Muhallab.
		4.	'Amrú bin Muslim *Al-Bahdlí.*
		5.	Junaíd bin 'Abd al raḥman *Al-Marrí* (under Hishám).
725–726	107	6.	Tamím bin Zaid *Al-'Utbí.*
		7.	Al ḥakim bin 'Awánah *Al-Kalbí.*
			('Amrú bin Muḥammad.)
			(Sulaimán bin Hishám and Abú Al-Khattáb)† under the 'Abbásides.

---

* Abu J'afir Aḥmad bin Yahya ibn Jábir al Balázarí, ob. inter 256 and 279 A.H., Ibn Khaldun, p. 438. Reinaud *Fragments Arabes et Persans inédits, relatifs à l'Inde*, pp. xviii., 182.

† Appendix to the *Arabs in Sind:* Cape Town, 1853. Elliot quoting "Tohfat ul Kirám," *Historians of India*, I., 443.

A.D.	A.H.		
		8.	'Abd al raḥman bin Muslin *'Al-Abdi* defeated by
		9.	Manṣúr bin Jamhúr *Al-Kalbi*, the local Governor under the Ummaíh Khalifs.
		10.	Músa bin K'aab, *Al-Tamimi*; overpowers Manṣúr. (The Tohfat ul Kirám attributes this victory to Dáúd bin 'Ali.)
757–8	140	11.	Hishám bin 'Amrú *Al-Taghlabi*.
		12.	'Amar bin Ḥafṣ bin 'Usmán, Hazármard.*
770–1	154	13.	Rúḥ bin Ḥátim.†
800	184	14.	Dáúd bin Yazíd bin Ḥátim.
		15.	Bashir bin Dáúd (about 200 A.H., Reinaud).
828	213‡	16.	Ghassán bin 'Abád.
		17.	Músa bin Yaḥia bin Khálid, *Al Barmaki* (dies in 221 A.H., 836 A.D.)
		18.	'Amrán bin Músa.§
		19.	Fazl bin Máhán.
		20.	Muḥammad bin Fazl, his brother Máhán rebels, and eventually The Native races regain possession of the soil.

In addition to the kingdoms of Manṣúrah and Multán there were other quasi independent governments at Bánia, where 'Umar the son of 'Abdal 'Azíz *Habbári* seems to have held sway,‖ and at Ḳasdár where the governor, in Ibn Haukal's time (A.D. 943) was Mu'ín bin Aḥmad.¶ But in all these cases, as indeed at Manṣúrah and Multán, the *Khutbah*, or public prayers, were read in the name of the Khalif.

I have one remark to make with reference to the peculiarly local characteristics of the numismatic remains discovered by Mr. Bellasis near the old site of Brahmanabad and the identification of the new town of Manṣúrah, as tested by the produce of the inhumed habitations hitherto penetrated, in the fact of the very limited number of Hindú coins found among the multitudes of medieval Muhammadan pieces, and that the former, as a rule, seem to have been casual contributions from other provinces, of no individual uniformity or appearance of age such as should connect them with the ancient Hindú capital.**

---

* Transferred from Sind to Africa in A.H. 151. Reinaud, p. 213.

† A.H. 160 to 161. Reinaud, p. 213.

‡ Gildemeister quoting Abulfida, II. 150.

§ Killed by عمر بن عبدالعزيز الهبادي Belázari, p. 215.

‖ Ibn Haukal, p. 231 text وبانية مدينة صغيرة ومنها عمر بن عبد العزيزالهباري القرشي

¶ Text معين بن احمد Gildemeister *De rebus Indicis*, Bonn., 1838, p. 171; Col. Anderson *Journ. As. Soc. Beng.*, 1852, p. 54; Elliot's *Historians*, vol. I. pp. 37, 38.

** The note which I compiled in 1858 to aid my first fragmentary description of the coins discovered by Mr. Bellasis at Brahmanábád, contains so many references that may prove useful to Antiquarians in Western India, that I have thought it advisable to correct and enlarge it, as far as possible, up to the requirements of the present day.

"Amrou, fils de Mohammed fils de Cassem . . . . . . fonda, en deçà du lac, une ville qu'il nomma Almansoura. C'est la ville où résident maintenant les gouverneurs."—p. 120. In a previous passage, Balázari tells us "Ensuite Mohammed fils de Cassem, se porta devant la vieille Bahmanábád, qui se trouvait à deux parasanges de Mansoura. Du reste Mansoura n'existait pas encore, et son emplacement actuel était alors un bois . . . . . Mohammed plaça un lieutenant à Bahmanábád; mais aujourd'hui la ville est ruinée."—"Balázari," Reinaud, *Fragments Arabes et Persans relatifs à l'Inde*, Paris, 1845, pp. 198, 211. The Arabian author from whom these traditions are derived, احمد بن يحيي البلاذري died in 279 A.H. (892 A.D.). See also Reinaud quoting Albírúní's "Tárikh-i-Hind," *Fragments*, p. 113. Ibn Khurdádbah (A.H. 260) المسالك وممالك text and translation by M. B. de Meynard, *Journal Asiatique*, 1865, pp. 277–8, 289, 292, &c. Sir H. Elliot's MS. of Albírúní's *Kánún* has the following:—بهمنوا و هي منه الكبري و سميت منصورة لان فاتحها قال نصرت Jaubert, in his translation of Edrisi, on the authority of original MSS., states that the local native

The first coin introduced into the following list is not supposed to belong to the province of Sind. It has been inserted here, with a view to trace the apparent prototype, upon which the arrangement of the reverse devices of the local coinage was based.

'Abd al Raḥman bin Muslim.

No. XVIII.* Copper. A.H. 133, 4, 5, 6. (A.D. 750–753, 4.)

Obverse	Reverse
لا اله ا لا الله وحده بسم الله مما امربه الامير عبد الرحمن بن مسلم سنة اربع وثلثين ومية	محمد ⋘ ⋙ رسول الله قل لا اسلكم ∴ عليه اجرا ∴ الا المودة ∴ في القربي
"*Nomine Dei. Est ex iis, quos (cudi) jussit Emirus 'Abd al Raḥman bin Muslim* (A.H.) 134."	"*Dic: non peto a vobis ullam hujus facti mercedem, nisi amorem in propinquos.*" (Ḳurán, 42. 22.)*

---

name of the place was مبرمان (variants, تامران, تاميرامان, and امامواد). Masúdi tell us, "I visited Multán after 300 A.H. when ابو الدلهات المنبه بن اسد القرشي السامي was king there." "At the same time I visited el Manṣúrah, the king of that country was then ابو المنذر عمر بن عبدالله [of the family of Habbár bin el Aswad]."—p. 385, Sprenger's Translation; M. Barbier de Meynard's edition, text and translation, Paris, 1861, vol. I. pp. 151, 372, 377, &c. With regard to the extent and importance of the kingdom we are informed that "All the estates and villages under the dependency of el-Manṣúrah amounted to 300,000; the whole country is well cultivated, and covered with trees and fields."—p. 386, *ibid.* Further references to the geographical and the other questions involved occur as follows:—Ḳodámah (ob. 337 A.H.), *Journal Asiatique*, 1862, p. 168; Vincent's *Commerce of the Ancients*, London, 1807, vol. I. p. 145; Gladwin's *Ayīn-i-Akbari*, vol. II. p. 137, *et seq.*; *Marásid-al-Ittila'*, vol. II. p. 161. "Istakhrí" (A.H. 300 to 309) "and Sind is the same as Manṣúrah . . . . Manṣúrah which they call Sindhi."—pp. 12 and 147; M. Goeje's new edition of the text, 1870, p. 171, *et seq.*; Ouseley's *Oriental Geography*, London, 1800. Ibn Haukal (A.H. 331 to 366).—M. Goeje's new edition of the text (Lugd. Bat., 1873), p. 226, *et seq.*; Gildemeister *de Rebus Indicis*, Bonn, 1838, p. 166; Col. Anderson's translation *Journ. As. Soc. Beng.*, vol. XXI. p. 42; *Liber Climatum*, Arabic text, J. H. Mœller, Gothæ, 1829; Sprenger's *Post- und Reiserouten des Orients*, Leipzig, 1864, pl. XIV. "Karte von Indien nach Byrúny"; Reinaud's *Géographie d'Aboulfeda*, vol. I. p. 386, &c.; *Tabari*, Paris ed., vol. III. p. 518; Reinaud's *Mémoire sur l'Inde*, pp. 169, 192, 235, &c.; *Ancient Accounts of India and China*, London, 1733; ditto, Reinaud's French edition, Paris, p. 212; Elliot's *Historians of India*, Calcutta, 1849; Elliot's *Appendix to the Arabs in Sind*, Cape Town, 1853. Most of the available information up to date has latterly been incorporated in vol. I. of Prof. Dowson's excellent edition of Elliot's *History of India, as told by its own Historians*, London, Trübner, 1867. *Ariana Antiqua*, p. 414; *Journ. As. Soc. Beng.*, vol. VII. pp. 93, 279; vol. X. p. 183; vol. XIV. p. 75; McMurdo, *Journ. R. As. Soc.*, vol. I. p. 23, *et seq.*; Burnes' *Bokhára*, vol. III. p. 31; Dr. Bird, *Journ. R. As. Soc.*, vol. I. p. 199; Postan's *Observations on Sindh*, p. 143; Pottinger's *Beloochistan and Sinde*, London, 1816, p. 381; Wood's *Oxus*, London, 1841, p. 20; Mohammed Ma'súm's *History of Sind*, A.D. 710 to 1590; *Bombay Government Selections*, New Series, No. XIII., 1855; Mr. A. F. Bellasis, *The Ruined City of Brahmanábád, in Sind*, Bombay, 1856; Col. Sykes in the *Illustrated London News*, Feb. 21 and Feb. 28, 1857, p. 187. With numerous illustrations of Brahmanábád and engravings of coins of Manṣúr bin Jamhur [No. XIX. of *this* series] and of Muhammad [No. XXII.]

* In Fræhn's Recensio (1826, p. 18) a second similar piece is given of the year 135 A.H., a new specimen of the same date is quoted by Stikel (Jena collection, 1845, p. 5). Tornberg cites a coin of 136 A.H. in his *Symbolæ ad Rem numariam Muhammedanorum* (Upsaliæ, 1856), p. 8; and finally M. Tiesenhausen produces a specimen bearing the date of A.H. 133, *Monnaies des Khalifes Orientaux* (St. Pétersbourg, 1873), pp. 65, 66.

Manṣúr the son of Jamhur, *Al Kalbí.*

No. XIX. Copper. Weight, 33 grains. Size, 6 of Mionnet's scale. Mr. Bellasis.
Manṣurah, A.H. ?

Obverse.	Reverse.
Area.	Area.
لا الـــه الا الله وحده لاشريك له	محمد  رسول الله
Margin.—Illegible.	Margin بسم الله ضرب [هذا الفلـ]س بالمنصورة مما امربه منصو . .
	"In the name of God, this copper coin was struck, at Manṣúrah, under the orders of Manṣú(r).

No. XX. Copper. Size, 4. Mr. Bellasis. Manṣúrah, A.H. ?

Obverse.	Reverse.
	Area.
Device.	محمد  رسول الله
Altogether effaced and obliterated.	Margin بسم [الله] ضرب هـ بالمنصورة مما امربه منصو . . .

'Abd ul-Raḥman.

No. XXI. Copper. Size, 5. Weight, 44 grains.

Obverse.—Central device, a *star,* reduced to four points,  on the sides of which are disposed, in the form of a square, the words محمد رسول الله عبدالرحمن The outer margin of the piece displays a line of dots enclosed within two plain circles, with four small dotted semicircles to fill in the space left vacant by the angular central legend.

Reverse.—A scalloped square, surrounded by dots, within which, arranged in three lines, are the words, بالله عبدالرحمن لسلعار ; the concluding word I am unable to decipher, it is possibly the name of 'Abdulraḥman's tribe.

When the English government originated a "Star of India," they were perhaps not aware that Sind had a star of its own; a very special and discriminative symbol, which attained such permanent recognition in and around the province itself, that the device here discovered on 'Abdulraḥman's coins, continued to constitute, in a slightly modified form, the typical emblem of the state, down to the time of Táj-ud-dín Ilduz, the lieutenant of Muhammad bin Sám, eventually independent *Sultán* of Sind, and likewise that of his opponent and successor Kubáchah, another general of the *Ghorí* conquerors of India, who established himself in Sind about 600 A.H. (1203–4 A.D.) to fall at last before the troops of the chivalric Jalál-ud-dín *Khárizmí*, who, in his turn had to swim the Indus for his life, before the hordes of Changís Khán.*

Muḥammad.

No. XXII. Copper. Size, 3.

A unique coin of apparently similar type, (though the obverse is, in this case, absolutely blank,) replaces the name of 'Abd-ul-raḥman on the reverse by that of محمد Muḥammad. The concluding tribal term seems to be identical with the designation embodied in the Kufic scroll at the foot of the reverse of No. XXI.

'Abdallah.

No. XXIII. Copper.

Obverse.—Device as in No. XXI. ('Abd-ul-raḥman).

Legend : محمد [رسول الله] عبدالله

Reverse.—Blank.

No. XXIV. Copper. Size, 3½. Weight 18 grains.

Obverse.—Central device the conventional four-pointed star, as in No. XXI., around which, in a circular scroll, may be partially read the formula لا اله الا الله وحده لاشريک له.

Reverse.—Central device composed of the name of عبدالله *Abd-allah*; the two portions عبد and الله being crossed at right angles, so as to form a *tughra* or monogrammic imitation of the outline of the star with four points of the obverse device.

The marginal legend is arranged in the form of a square, and consists of the words محمد رسول الله [الا]مير

No. XXV. Silver. Size, 2. Weight, 8·4 grains.†

Palm branches, roses, stars, and all other mundane devices are rejected and replaced by simple Kufic legends, so cherished by severe Muhammadans, to the following effect :

Obverse.— لااله الا الله وحده لاشريک له

Reverse.— محمد رسول الله الامير عبدالله

No. XXVa. Copper, bearing similar legends. Other specimens vary in the division of the words, and omit the title of *Al-Amír*.

---

* Ilduz's special symbol was a "star" beneath the conventional figure of the Rájpút horseman. See coin No. 24, p. 31, of My *Patháṅ Kings of Delhi*, Trübner, 1871. Kubáchah follows in the occasional use of the Star, No. 87, p. 101, *ibid.*; so also Muhammad bin Sám's *own* coin, No. 7. (Prinsep's *Essays*, pl. XXVI. fig. 45,) and Altamsh's coin, No. 48, continue to display the local device. The coins of Uzbeg Páí, the Indian General of Jalálud-dín, Khárizmí struck at Multán, reproduce the identical cluster of the seven stars of the Sáh Kings, and the Guptas (plate VII. figs. 9-13 *ante*),—which discriminating mark survived, till lately, on the native currencies of Údipúr and Ujjain. *Patháṅ Kings of Delhi*, No. 85, p. 99; Prinsep's *Essays*, Useful Tables, No. 18, p. 67.

† Among the silver coins exhumed from the so-called Bráhmanábád, some are so minute as to weigh only 1·2 gr.

Banú-Dáúd. (Dáúd-putra's ?)*

No. XXVI. Silver. Weight, 5·6 grains. My Cabinet. Unpublished.

محمد رسول الله		بالله بنو د ا و د و ا صد

The archaic form of Ḳufic stamped on these coins, would, under ordinary circumstances have placed them in a far earlier position, in point of time, than their apparent associates in size and style, whose almost identical legends are couched in less monumental letters; but I prefer to attribute any divergence in this respect to local rather than epochal influences, regarding which we have had so many instructive lessons in the parallel Nágarí alphabets of India.†

Banú-'Umar.‡

No. XXVII. Silver. Size, 1½. Weight, 9 grains. *Five specimens.* Mr. Bellasis.

Obverse.—Legends arranged in five lines.

بالله محمد رسول الله عمر

Marginal lines, plain or dotted, complete the piece.

Reverse.—Ḳufic legends in three lines.

‡بالله بنو عمروية منذر

No. XXVIII. Copper. Size, 4. Weight, 35 grains. Common.

Legends as in the silver coins, with the exception that the بنو is placed, for economy of space, in the opening between the two ل's of بالله.

No. XXIX. Copper. Size, 3½. Weight, 21 grains. *Unique.* Mr. Bellasis.
Manṣúrah, A.H. . . 4.

Obverse.—Blank. Reverse.—

Centre : بنو . . . . عمروية منذر

Margin : . . . . س بالمنصورة سنة اربع . . . . ?

---

* Dáúd-putras, *Journ. R. As. Soc.*, vol. VII. p. 27.

† The patronymic, in its local application, may have been derived from *the* Dáúd bin 'Alí bin 'Abbás No. 10 in the above list (p. 57), who was so prominently associated with the overthrow of the 'Ummaih Khalifs. (Tabari IV. pp. 289, 326, 342.) As uncle of the new Khalif he was all powerful, and as governor of Kufah (in A.H. 132), of which Sind was a dependency, *his troops* would naturally have effected the final transfer of dominion in that province. Mas'audi VI. pp. 88, 91, 98; price II. pp. 2, 4.

‡ I am inclined to identify this ruler with the *Abúl Manżar* 'Umar bin Abdallah, indicated in the general note p. 58 *ante*, as the reigning sovereign of Manṣúrah, in A.H. 300– , at the period of the geographer M'asúdí's visit to the valley of the Indus, and of whom he speaks further in the following terms:—"There is some relationship between the royal family of el-Manṣúrah and the family of esh-Shawárib, the Kadi, ال ابي الشوارب القاضي for the kings of el-Manṣúrah are of the family of Habbár ben el-Aswad, هبار بن الاسود and have the name of Beni 'Amr ben 'Abd el-Azíz el-Karshí, بني عمر بن عبد العزيز القرشي who is to be distinguished from 'Amr ben 'Abd el-Azíz ben Merwán, the Omaïyide (Khalif)".—Sprenger's *Meadow of Gold*, p. 385. The Arabic is from M. B. de Meynard's edition, p. 377. See also Gildemeister, quoting *Ibn Haukal*, p. 166; and Elliot, citing the same author (*Historians of India*), p. 63; and Professor Dowson's edition, vol. I. pp. 21.

Banú 'Umar.

No. XXX. Copper. Size, 4½. Weight, 36 grains. Unique. Sir Bartle Frere.

Obverse.—Central device, four lines crossing each other at a common centre, so as to form a species of star of eight points; four of these are, however, rounded off by dots.

Legend, arranged as a square:

محمد رسول الله سر

with single dots at the corner angles, and two small circles filling in the vacant spaces outside of each word.

Margin.—Two plain circular lines, with an outer circle of dots.

Reverse.—Central legends in three lines within a triple circle composed of dots, circlets, and an inner plain line. I transcribe the legend, with due reservation, as:

بالله بنو عمروية منذر

Aḥmad.

No. XXXI. Silver. Mr. Burgess. Unpublished.

Obverse.

لا اله الا
الله وحده
لاشريك له

Reverse.

محمد
رسول
الله الامير
احمد

'Abd-allah (*Wali* and *Malik.*)

No. XXXII. Silver. New varieties. Mr. Burgess. Unpublished.

Obverse.

محمد
رسول
الله
عبدالله

Reverse.

بالله ولي
عبدالله
وملك

In terminating this brief Muhammadan section, I ought to advert, momentarily, to the information obtained from the early Arabian travellers in India, respecting the mixed currencies of Sind and the adjoining provinces.

The Merchant Sulaimán, A.H. 237 (A.D. 851), is the first who affords us any insight into the condition of the *circulating media* of the land; he tells us that, among other pieces used in commerce in the dominions of the *Balhará*, *Ṭátariya* dirhams took a prominent place, and that these were reckoned in value as equal to 1½ of the ordinary coins of the King.*

---

* Abú Zaid, circâ 303 A.H. who follows Sulaimán, incidentally mentions: "Autrefois, l'on portait dans l'Inde les dinárs du Sind (وكان يحمل الي الهند في القديم الدنانير السندية) dont chacun équivalait à trois dinárs ordinaires et davantage,"—(وما زاد) p. 153, Reinaud's translation.

So, later in point of time, the Egyptian author of the Masálik-al-Abṣár refers to the "*Tankah* d'or" as equal to 3 *Mithkals*. This was the modern representative of the normal ancient weight of 100 Ratis, (*Ṣataraktika*,) or, as nearly as possible, 175 grains. See My *Pathan Kings*, pp. 217 *et seq.*, and My *Ancient Indian Weights*, pp. 12, 36, 70.

The identification of this term *Ṭátariya*, has formed the subject of much vague speculation; M. Reinaud's latest conjecture pointed at a derivation from the Greek *στατήρ, Stater.**

I myself have, for long past, persistently held that the true term was to be found in *Ṭáhiriya*, the name of a dynasty dominant above all others in Eastern Asia at the period of the Merchant's visit to India.†

This conclusion has gradually been strengthened by the discovery of the exact generic *word* in the unique Oxford MS. text of Ibn Khurdádbah,‡ and in the more critical version of Mas'audi,§ lately completed in Paris.

To these evidences, I am now able to add the definite legend of a coin of Ṭalḥah bin Ṭáhir, struck at Bust, on the Helmund, in A.H. 209 (A.D. 824).

Ṭalḥah bin Ṭáhir, A.H. 209.

Copper: size, 5½; weights, 30, 31, and 22·5 grains. Bust. A.H. 209 (A.D. 824). Two specimens, Cunningham collection, B.M. A third coin, recently acquired, by the B. M., contributes the legible name of the Mint.‖

Obverse.—

Centre :— لا اله الا الله وحده لاشريك له

Margin :— بسم الله ضرب هذا الفلس ببست سنة تسع و ماتين

Reverse.—Central device, a reduced Sassanian head, to the right, with the usual flowing back-hair, and traces of the conventional wings above the cap; the border of the robe is bossed or beaded.

In front of the profile the name of الطلحة is inserted.

Margin :— محمد رسول الله مما امربه الامير طلحة علي يدي عبدالله

This coin has further claims upon our attention, in its testimony to the survival of old types and the continuity of the recognition of Sassanian devices in Seistán, extending, in its local influences, even to the confessed followers of Islám, up to so late a period as 209 years after the Hijerah of Muhammad.

---

* "La monnaie qui circule dans ses États consiste en pièces d'argent, qu'on nomme *thatherya*, الطاطرية. Chacune de ces pièces équivaut à un dirhem et demi, monnaie du souverain." *Relation des Voyages*, Paris, 1845, I. p. 25; Reinaud, *L'Inde*, 1849, p. 235; Gildemeister, *de Rebus Indicis*, Bonn, 1838, p. 166; Tod's *Rajasthan*, quoted in Prinsep's Essays, I. 86. Dr. Sprenger, in his edition of Mas'audi, proposes the interpretation of *Ṭalatawiya*.

† The Arabic text of Y'aḳúbí, edited by Juynboll (Lugd. Bat., 1861), gives the dates of this family as follows:—

Ṭáhir bin Al Ḥusain - - -	A.H. 205	A.D. 820–1
Ṭalḥah bin Ṭáhir - - -	A.H. 207	A.D. 822–3
'Abdallah bin Ṭáhir - - -	A.H. 215	A.D. 830
Ṭáhir bin 'Abdallah - - -	A.H. 230	A.D. 844–5
Muḥammad bin Ṭáhir - - -	A.H. 248	A.D. 862–3
Y'aḳúb bin Laiś - - - -	A.H. 259	A.D. 872–3

See also Prinsep's *Essays*, U. T., p. 304; *Hamza Iṣfahání* (Gottwaldt), pp. 177, 228, &c., &c.

‡ *Journ. Asiatique*, 1865, p. 289. M. B. de Meynard, I find, adhered to the *Tatherides*, in defiance of Professor Cowell's testimony to *Ṭaheriya*. Elliot's *Historians*, vol. I. p. 4.

§ Text, vol. I. p. 382.

‖ Mr. S. L. Poole discovered the correct reading of this mint from a later coin of *Lais bin 'Ali*, A.H. 298. N.C. vol. XIII. p. 169.

Considered under this aspect of fixity of national designs, it may instruct us in the classification of some of the devices previously noticed,* about which our knowledge is at present indeterminate in the extreme. We know from the later developments of the Indo-Muhammadan coinages of the immediate successors of Mahmúd of Ghazní,† that the Eastern *Turkí* Muslims were less strict in their denunciations of emblems and figures, than their presumedly more orthodox co-religionists of the West, and that in these cases the Northern invaders of India freely accepted the national types of the conquered kingdoms, which in this sense may furnish data for tracing back and discriminating the earlier examples of parallel assimilations.

To return to the material estimates of the *Sindí* currencies, we are in a position to cite the consecutive testimony of Iṣtakhrí and Ibn Ḥaukal, whose verbatim texts in their latest exhaustive form are reproduced in the foot-note.† These restored versions authorize us to infer that there were, among other impinging or still extant national methods of weighing and estimating metallic values *inter se*, certain market rates, or prices current, for international exchanges, which were quoted in fractions at that time, as our half-crowns still count, in defiance of decimals, in the London stock lists.

From these returns we gather that there were coins termed "Victorious" equivalent to five ordinary dirhams in the local exchange, and that, concurrently the *Bázár* or open market recognized a totally different scale, based upon a coinage only *plus* ⅛th or ⅓rd above the home issues.

With the very imperfect numismatic materials extant, it would be presumptuous to pretend to fix, even approximately, the coin weights and measures obtaining in such a vague international crossway as Manṣúrah; but I could quote within narrow geographical or epochal limits, such extreme variations of weights of dinárs, dirhams and copper coins a discretion, that, if I wished it, I might prove almost any given sum to momentary demonstration, an exercise which, as a collector of positive facts, I specially desire to avoid.

---

* p. 26 *ante*.

† Prinsep's *Essays*, vol. I. p. 333; *Pathân Kings of Delhi*, p. 58; *Journ. R. As. Soc.*, vol. XVII. pp. 171, 177.

Iṣtakhrí,—ونقودهم القاهريّات كلّ درهم نحو خمسة دراهم ولهم درهم يقال له الطاطريّ في الدرهم وزن درهم وثلثين

Ibn Ḥaukal.—ونقودهم القندهاريات كلّ درهم منها خمسة دراهم ولهم درهم يقال له الطاطري في الدرهم درهم وثمن

The conversion of the *Ḳaheriya* into *Ḳandahāriya* seems to have been a purely arbitrary correction, and one not justified by the tenor of the associate text.

Kandahár is not mentioned elsewhere in Ibn Ḥauḳal's geographical lists. The town at this period does not appear to have attained any degree of importance. See Goeje's text, p. 297. The name, however, occurs in Ibn Khordádbah, IV., p. 278.